ELEMENTS OF ENGLISH POETRY

Oksun Kang · Steven Reeder

Shinasa

이 저서는 2010년 동서대학교 학술연구비 지원으로 제작되었습니다.

ELEMENTS OF ENGLISH POETRY

Contents

Prologue

Poetry is art that increases in pleasure the more you study the form. Words on a blank page are like colored paint on a canvas—anyone can do it—but only the true artist can do it well. When you walk into a museum to view a Jackson Pollock painting, you may wonder what makes it art, and you may wonder correctly. You may open this book and read e.e. cummings "in just—"; then wonder why it is poetry. You may also think that anyone could write a poem like that. The answer to that response is that anyone *can* write poetry if that person truly understands the elements of poetry.

Reading this text will help you explore twelve different elements of poetry that are used by the poet to make verse richer and more fulfilling. When you finish this book, it is our, the editors, wish that you will never look at a published poem and ask, "Why is this a poem?" It is our hope that you will better appreciate the art form that is poetry, and that every reading enriches your life. Perhaps you will even start to write poetry yourself.

The book has been divided into twelve chapters focusing on an individual element of poetry. Each element has an introductory explanation of how to better understand the element by focusing on several different poems or stanzas of poems. To better help you understand the more difficult words with multiple meanings or the more archaic words no longer in use, footnotes have been provided with each poem. In the Appendix, we have provided study questions for each poem to help you practice the concepts introduced at the beginning of each element. They can be used for class assignments or just to get you thinking about the poem. They are not the only questions you should ask while reading, but they do try to get you started. As a further study aid, a recording of three poems from each chapter has been provided to help you understand how the poem sounds. To better give you an overarching sample of poems, no poet was repeated for the recordings.

It is our goal for this book to help aid your further interest in poetry. It is only a basic introduction, and the selections of poems are what we found to be the most creative in the English language. We were also limited to those poems found in the public domain. This meant that they had to be published before 1923. Unfortunately, many talented twentieth century poets could not be included in this volume. Their voices will be missed.

We would encourage you to take what you have learned here and read other books with new eyes of enjoyment, that you see poems as a great work of art, aware of all the intricate rhythm, rhyme, and metaphors layered throughout. We hope that you relish them as the key to understanding human nature, knowledge, and experience.

Steven Reeder
Dongseo University

ELEMENT *ONE*:
VOICE

Introduction to Element One: Voice

When reading poetry, we need to understand foremost that the **speaker**'s voice and the poet's, with rare exceptions, are not the same persona. Thus, when we read poetry, we need to ask, "Who is the speaker?" The answer is rarely the poet. We must also ask, "To whom is he or she speaking?" There will be times when the speaker is referenced in the title or in the actual poem and could be a historical or mythological persona; other times he or she will be the "I" speaking directly to us or another persona in the poem. The "I" is sometimes used as the autobiographical "I", where confessions are made and secrets are revealed. It is important to remember that the poet and the speaker are separate. We must never assume that the speaker of the poem is bearing the thoughts and feelings of the poet but only those of the persona the poet is assuming in writing the poem.

The speaker's voice is manifested through words read or heard, and voice expresses **tone**. What is tone exactly? It is the poet's stance toward the subject and audience as hinted by the poem itself. In order to understand tone, we should focus on the speaker's "tone of voice" as we would experience it in actual conversation. The speaker may express happiness, anger, awe, respect, or hatred, among a plethora of other emotions. Thus, we must view more than just the words of the speaker, but also the intent. "Thank God, you're here!" can be expressed in a tone of thankfulness, but also sarcastically to barely hide disappointment. To understand tone, we must look past the words and into the world or setting of the poem. In a conversation, the listener depends on not only the words spoken, but the voice, facial expressions, and body language to make sense of the speaker's meaning. A reader of poetry must become just as proficient with the clues given by the poet. Tone is found in the very language of the poem through the use or neglect of meter and rhyme, details, words, sentence patterns, imagery, and figurative language. All of these various elements of poetry will be discussed in each of the following chapters.

As an example of speaker and tone, let's look at a few lines from Stephen Crane's poem "War is Kind."

> Do not weep, babe, for war is kind.
> Because your father tumbled in the yellow trenches,
> Raged at his breast, gulped and died,
> Do not weep.
> War is kind.

Taking the title, the first, and last sentence of the stanza, the speaker paints a positive picture of war, yet we must look at the overall context of the poem. The speaker also mentions the father falling in the trenches of World War I where he is gassed in the trenches by the German's chemical agent sulfur mustard that gives off a yellowish color. There, in the trenches, his father dies, gasping for breath, and eventually suffocates. But he is not to worry, for war is kind. How is the reader supposed to react to this stanza? We can see that the speaker does not literally mean that war is kind, but is speaking with tongue in cheek while listing the most horrendous atrocities that occurred during the Great War. This is what it means to focus on tone. Irony, in this case, is easy to spot.

The meaning of a poem is found by paying close attention to the speaker's voice and the poem's language that was written to express a certain tone and feeling. These nuggets of language and nuance are placed in the poem by the poet for the reader to experience through multiple readings. Let's examine a stanza from John Donne's poem "The Flea."

> Mark but his flea, and mark in this,
> How little that which thou deny'st me is;
> It sucked me first, and now sucks thee,
> And in this flea our two bloods mingled be;

Thou know'st that this cannot be said
A sin, nor shame, nor loss of maidenhead,
  Yet this enjoys before it woo[1],
  And pampered[2] swells with one blood made of two,
  And this, alas, is more than we would do.

We start to understand the tone of the poem as being desperate with the word "deny'st" (denied). The speaker is showing a flea that has just bitten him to a certain woman of his desire to whom it has now jumped to, and he tries to convince her that the loss of her virginity (maidenhead) will be no more sinful or shameful as the flea mixing his blood with hers. A common theory in the 16th century was that sexual intercourse was the mixing of male and female blood. The language turns playful in the tercet (three lined stanza; see chapter 10), where the speaker tells his lady that the flea enjoys the mixing of blood without a formal wooing (which is what is doing), and if such a mixing of blood has not bothered her, then how could their own love making be any different? Sly words! The next stanza continues:

Oh stay, three lives in one flea spare,
Where we almost, yea[3] more than married are,
This flea is you and I, and this
Our marriage bed, and marriage temple is;
Though parents grudge, and you, we're met,
And cloistered[4] in these living walls of jet[5].
    Though use make you apt to kill me,
    Let not to that, self-murder added be,
    And sacrifice, three sins in killing three.

Here the tone becomes more playful and absurd. The speaker tells the maiden that since they have become "one flesh" in the flea, they

1 woo: *v.* to attract the love of another
2 pampered: *adj.* old form meaning 'to eat a lot'
3 yea: *adv.* old form meaning 'indeed'
4 cloister: *v.* to confine, especially in a monastery; virgins were often sent to monasteries to protect their virginity.
5 jet: *adj.* black; the color of the fleas carapace

are, practically speaking, married; thus, in all legal and moral terms, they have right to have sex without shame. The maiden's prompt reply is to squish the flea with her finger as revealed by his suddenly exclamation, "Oh stay," as in "stay your hand from squishing the flea." The speaker's use of religious imagery with words such as "temple," "cloistered," and "walls of jet," expresses that their act of love making would have the full blessing of God, for to deny the speaker his need for such is to commit heresy; she is denying the very primal urge to be whole again, which is how the speaker views their joining. The speaker adds in the third stanza.

> Cruel and sudden, has thou since
> Purpled thy nail, in blood of innocence?
> Wherein could this flea guilty be,
> Except in that drop it sucked from thee?

Here the humorous and playful tone of the poem comes to the fore when the speaker laments the maiden's squishing of the flea. The words "cruel and sudden" are seen as ironic and playful as she stains her nail with the flea's blood (which is purple). He claims this is similar to murder since both their blood resides in the flea. Because killing the flea and committing sacrilege was so simple, then it should be just as easy to give into his demands for love making.

Are we then to read this poem as the poet John Donne's desire to woo the reader or some woman in his church? Of course not. First of all, John Donne was a respected preacher and held a leading position in the Church of England. We are to read the poem as a **dramatic monologue**, which is poetry that offers substantial insight into the mind of the speaker. In this case, it is the mind of a rake, who is so desperately trying to woo a woman, that opens up to us so that we can see how absurd his reasoning actually is. Through the study of voice, we can come to understand more fully the personality and character of the speaker as being separate from the poet.

MY LAST DUCHESS

Robert Browning 1812-1889

Ferrara

That's my last duchess painted on the wall,
Looking as if she were alive. I call
That piece a wonder, now: Frà[1] Pandolf's hands
Worked busily a day, and there she stands.
Will't please you sit and look at her? I said
"Frà Pandolf" by design, for never read
Strangers like you that pictured countenance,
The depth and passion of its earnest glance,
But to myself they turned (since none puts by
The curtain I have drawn for you, but I)
And seemed as they would ask me, if they durst[2],
How such a glance came there; so, not the first
Are you to turn and ask thus. Sir, 'twas not
Her husband's presence only, called that spot
Of joy into the Duchess' cheek: perhaps
Frà Pandolf chanced to say "Her mantle[3] laps[4]
"Over my lady's wrist too much," or "Paint
"Must never hope to reproduce the faint
"Half-flush that dies along her throat": such stuff
Was courtesy, she thought, and cause enough
For calling up that spot of joy. She had
A heart how shall I say? too soon made glad,

1 Fra: *n.* a friar in the Roman Catholic Church
2 durst: *v.* old form meaning 'dared'
3 mantle: *n.* a cape or cloak
4 lap: *v.* to hang over

Too easily impressed; she liked whate'er
She looked on, and her looks went everywhere.
Sir, 'twas all one! My favor at her breast,
The dropping of the daylight in the West,
The bough of cherries some officious[5] fool
Broke in the orchard for her, the white mule
She rode with round the terrace all and each
Would draw from her alike the approving speech,
Or blush, at least. She thanked men good! but thanked
Somehow I know not how as if she ranked
My gift of a nine-hundred-years-old name
With anybody's gift. Who'd stoop to blame
This sort of trifling? Even had you skill
In speech which I have not to make your will
Quite clear to such an one, and say, "Just this
"Or that in you disgusts me; here you miss,
"Or there exceed the mark" and if she let
Herself be lessoned so, nor plainly set
Her wits to yours, forsooth[6], and make excuse,
E'en then would be some stooping; and I choose
Never to stoop. Oh sir, she smiled, no doubt,
Whene'er I passed her; but who passed without
Much the same smile? This grew; I gave commands;
Then all smiles stopped together. There she stands
As if alive. Will't please you rise? We'll meet
The company below, then. I repeat,
The Count your master's known munificence[7]
Is ample warrant that no just pretense
Of mine for dowry[8] will be disallowed;

5 officious: *adj.* eager to serve
6 forsooth: *adv.* old form meaning 'in truth'
7 munificence: *n.* generosity

Though his fair daughter's self, as I avowed[9]
At starting, is my object. Nay we'll go
Together down, sir. Notice Neptune[10], though,
Taming a sea-horse, thought a rarity,
Which Claus of Innsbruck cast in bronze for me!

8 dowry: *n.* money that the bride's family gives to the groom
9 avow: *v.* declare
10 Neptune: *n.* Roman god of the sea; Poseidon is the Greek name

THE RIGHTS OF WOMEN

Anne Laetitia Barbauld 1743-1825

Yes, injured Woman! rise, assert thy right!
Woman! too long degraded, scorned, opprest;
O born to rule in partial Law's despite,
Resume thy native empire o'er the breast!

Go forth arrayed in panoply[1] divine;
That angel pureness which admits no stain;
Go, bid proud Man his boasted rule resign,
And kiss the golden scepter of thy reign.

Go, gird[2] thyself with grace; collect thy store[3]
  Of bright artillery glancing from afar;
  Soft melting tones thy thundering cannon's roar,
  Blushes and fears thy magazine of war.

Thy rights are empire: urge no meaner claim,—
Felt, not defined, and if debated, lost;
Like sacred mysteries, which withheld from fame,
Shunning discussion, are revered the most.

Try all that wit and art suggest to bend
Of thy imperial foe the stubborn knee;
Make treacherous Man thy subject, not thy friend;
Thou mayst command, but never canst be free.

---

1 panoply: *n.* a suit of armor
2 gird: *v.* strengthen
3 store: *n.* supply

Awe the licentious[4], and restrain the rude;
Soften the sullen, clear the cloudy brow:
Be, more than princes' gifts, thy favors sued[5];—
She hazards all, who will the least allow.

But hope not, courted idol of mankind,
On this proud eminence secure to stay;
Subduing and subdued, thou soon shalt[6] find
Thy coldness soften, and thy pride give way.

Then, then, abandon each ambitious thought,
Conquest or rule thy heart shall feebly move,
In Nature's school, by her soft maxims taught,
That separate rights are lost in mutual love.

4 licentious: *n.* lewd; sexually unrestrained
5 sue: *v.* to petition
6 shalt: *v.* old form meaning 'shall'

ON MY FIRST SON

Ben Jonson 1572-1637

Farewell, thou child of my right hand, and joy;
    My sin was too much hope of thee, loved boy.
Seven years thou wert[1] lent to me, and I thee pay.
    Exacted by the fate, on the just day.
Oh, could I lose all father now! For why
    Will man lament the state he should envy?
To have so soon 'scaped[2] world's and flesh's rage,
    And, if no other misery, yet age?
Rest in soft peace, and asked, say here doth lie
    Ben Jonson his best piece of poetry;
For whose sake, henceforth, all his vows be such,
    As what he loves may never like too much.

1 wert: *v.* old form meaning 'was'

2 'scaped: *v.* escaped; to fit the meter the poet cut off the first syllable

O CAPTAIN! MY CAPTAIN!

Walt Whitman 1819-1892

O Captain! my Captain! our fearful trip is done,
The ship has weathered every rack[3], the prize we sought is won,
The port is near, the bells I hear, the people all exulting[4],
While follow eyes the steady keel[5], the vessel grim and daring;
  But O heart! heart! heart!
   O the bleeding drops of red,
    Where on the deck my Captain lies,
     Fallen cold and dead.

O Captain! my Captain! rise up and hear the bells;
Rise up—for you the flag is flung for you the bugle trills[6],
For you bouquets and ribbon'd wreaths—for you the shores a-crowding,
For you they call, the swaying mass, their eager faces turning;
  Here Captain! dear father!
   This arm beneath your head!
    It is some dream that on the deck,
     You've fallen cold and dead.

My Captain does not answer, his lips are pale and still;
My father does not feel my arm, he has no pulse nor will;
The ship is anchored safe and sound, its voyage closed and done;
From fearful trip the victor ship comes in with object won;

3 rack: *n.* violent twist
4 exulting: *v.* rejoicing
5 keel: *n.* often referred to as a ship in literature
6 trill: *v.* to call out

Exult O shores, and ring O bells!
  But I, with mournful tread,
    Walk the deck my Captain lies,
      Fallen cold and dead.

THE LOVE SONG OF J. ALFRED PRUFROCK

T.S. Eliot 1888-1965

s'io credesse che mia risposta fosse
A persona che mai tornasse al mondo,
Questa fiamma staria senza piu scosse.
Ma perciocche giammai di questo fondo
Non torno vivo alcun, s'i'odo il vero,
Senza tema d'infamia ti rispondo[1].

Let us go then, you and I,
When the evening is spread out against the sky
Like a patient etherized[2] upon a table;
Let us go, through certain half-deserted streets,
The muttering retreats
Of restless nights in one-night cheap hotels
And sawdust restaurants with oyster-shells:
Streets that follow like a tedious argument
Of insidious intent
To lead you to an overwhelming question…
Oh, do not ask, "What is it?"
Let us go and make our visit.

In the room the women come and go
Talking of Michelangelo[3].

---

1 The following is translated from the original Italian as found in Dante's Inferno XXVII, 61-66:
If I thought my answer were given
To anyone who would ever return to the world,
This flame would stand still without moving any further.
But since never from this abyss
Has anyone ever returned alive, if what I hear is true,
Without fear of infamy I answer you.

2 etherized: *v.* to be put under anesthesia

3 Michelangelo: (1475–1564) Italian artist

The yellow fog that rubs its back upon the window-panes,
The yellow smoke that rubs its muzzle[4] on the window-panes
Licked its tongue into the corners of the evening,
Lingered upon the pools that stand in drains,
Let fall upon its back the soot that falls from chimneys,
Slipped by the terrace, made a sudden leap,
And seeing that it was a soft October night,
Curled once about the house, and fell asleep.

And indeed there will be time
For the yellow smoke that slides along the street,
Rubbing its back upon the window-panes;
There will be time, there will be time
To prepare a face to meet the faces that you meet;
There will be time to murder and create,
And time for all the works and days of hands
That lift and drop a question on your plate;
Time for you and time for me,
And time yet for a hundred indecisions,
And for a hundred visions and revisions,
Before the taking of a toast and tea.

In the room the women come and go
Talking of Michelangelo.

And indeed there will be time
To wonder, "Do I dare?" and, "Do I dare?"
Time to turn back and descend the stair,
With a bald spot in the middle of my hair—
[They will say: "How his hair is growing thin!"]

---

4 muzzle: *n.* the jaws, mouth, and nose that extends from an animal's face

My morning coat, my collar mounting firmly to the chin,
My necktie rich and modest, but asserted by a simple pin—
[They will say: "But how his arms and legs are thin!"]
Do I dare
Disturb the universe?
In a minute there is time
For decisions and revisions which a minute will reverse.

For I have known them all already, known them all—
Have known the evenings, mornings, afternoons,
I have measured out my life with coffee spoons;
I know the voices dying with a dying fall
Beneath the music from a farther room.
    So how should I presume?

And I have known the eyes already, known them all—
The eyes that fix you in a formulated phrase,
And when I am formulated, sprawling on a pin,
When I am pinned and wriggling on the wall,
Then how should I begin
To spit out all the butt-ends of my days and ways?
    And how should I presume?

And I have known the arms already, known them all—
Arms that are braceleted and white and bare
[But in the lamplight, downed with light brown hair!]
Is it perfume from a dress
That makes me so digress?
Arms that lie along a table, or wrap about a shawl.
    And should I then presume?
    And how should I begin?

. . . . .

Shall I say, I have gone at dusk through narrow streets
And watched the smoke that rises from the pipes
Of lonely men in shirt-sleeves, leaning out of windows? ···

I should have been a pair of ragged claws
Scuttling across the floors of silent seas.

. . . . .

And the afternoon, the evening, sleeps so peacefully!
Smoothed by long fingers,
Asleep··· tired··· or it malingers[5],
Stretched on the floor, here beside you and me.
Should I, after tea and cakes and ices,
Have the strength to force the moment to its crisis?
But though I have wept and fasted, wept and prayed,
Though I have seen my head [grown slightly bald] brought in
  upon a platter,
I am no prophet[6]—and here's no great matter;
I have seen the moment of my greatness flicker,
And I have seen the eternal Footman hold my coat, and snicker,
And in short, I was afraid.

And would it have been worth it, after all,
After the cups, the marmalade, the tea,
Among the porcelain, among some talk of you and me, to
  pretend sickness, esp. in order to shirk one's duty, avoid work
Would it have been worth while,

5 malinger: *v.* to pretend to be sick to avoid performing a duty

6 Though I have seen my head...I am no prophet: this statement refers to the prophet John the Baptist who was beheaded by Herod Antipas and had his head offered upon a platter to Salome.

To have bitten off the matter with a smile,
To have squeezed the universe into a ball
To roll it toward some overwhelming question,
To say: "I am Lazarus,[7] come from the dead,
Come back to tell you all, I shall tell you all"—
If one, settling a pillow by her head,
    Should say: "That is not what I meant at all.
    That is not it, at all."

And would it have been worth it, after all,
Would it have been worth while,
After the sunsets and the dooryards and the sprinkled streets,
After the novels, after the teacups, after the skirts that trail along
  the floor—
And this, and so much more?—
It is impossible to say just what I mean!
But as if a magic lantern threw the nerves in patterns on a screen:
Would it have been worth while
If one, settling a pillow or throwing off a shawl,
And turning toward the window, should say:
    "That is not it at all,
    That is not what I meant, at all."

. . . . .

No! I am not Prince Hamlet[8], nor was meant to be;
Am an attendant lord, one that will do
To swell a progress, start a scene or two,

7 Lazarus: a man whom Jesus miraculously raised from the dead

8 Hamlet: a fictional prince of Denmark in Shakespeare's play who deals with madness over the death of his father and seeks to avenge his death only to cause the deaths of his close friends and loved ones. In the wake of all the deaths, Hamlet is finally the last to die.

Advise the prince; no doubt, an easy tool,
Deferential[9], glad to be of use,
Politic, cautious, and meticulous;
Full of high sentence, but a bit obtuse[10];
At times, indeed, almost ridiculous—
Almost, at times, the Fool.

I grow old··· I grow old···
I shall wear the bottoms of my trousers rolled.

Shall I part my hair behind? Do I dare to eat a peach?
I shall wear white flannel trousers, and walk upon the beach.
I have heard the mermaids singing, each to each.

I do not think that they will sing to me.

I have seen them riding seaward on the waves
Combing the white hair of the waves blown back
When the wind blows the water white and black.

We have lingered in the chambers of the sea
By sea-girls wreathed with seaweed red and brown
Till human voices wake us, and we drown.

9 deferential: *adj.* respectful
10 obtuse: *adj.* slow in thought

ELEMENT *TWO*:
THEME

Introduction to Element Two: Theme

Reading poetry forces us to think about familiar experiences from a different perspective. **Theme,** which deals with the overall meaning, or the central idea, of a poem, should be the first element of poetry you are aware of in your attempt to tackle the overall meaning. A poetic theme deals with an abstraction (such as war) that materializes through how a person, action, or image is represented in the poem (war is destructive through loss of innocence and life). Do not think of a theme as merely a topic or action. A theme is more than a simple subject, like love, war, or religion; a theme is both a subject and a predicate. Thus, the theme of Stephen Crane's "War is Kind" is not just "war," which is merely the topic of a poem, but "war seems heroic but is not because of the destruction of lives and society" is the theme because it explicitly turns an abstract concept into a deeper meaning.

Theme also deals with concepts. For example, what draws us to a particular poem? To answer that question is to address the theme. Does the poem make us think? Does it offer us a new perspective? Does it help us create any new ideas on a subject? Whatever the poem does, it creates a moment in time to ponder certain issues or remember ideals of the past. If we try reading a poem with distractions around us, we will soon realize that it is hard to understand. We need to find a nice quiet place to read, and then let the ideas flow through us. Soon the poem starts to make sense, not only on a thematic level, but also on a personal level as well.

We must be careful when reading poems that we do not narrow-mindedly settle on just a general theme or subject; that may miss the whole point of the poem—the predicate of the sentence. Poetry anthologies may collect individual poems under the universal **subjects** of love, war, personal identity, solitude, or art. When reading poems of war, some may be eulogizing the dead, celebrating a famous victory, condemning wanton destruction of life and property, or even pondering a quiet moment during the march to battle. However, the **abstract** theme of war is not all that the poem has to offer. To understand the depth of theme, let's analyze Rupert Brooke's war poem "The Soldier" for theme.

If I should die, think only this of me:
  That there's some corner of a foreign field
That is for ever England. There shall be
  In that rich earth a richer dust concealed;
A dust whom England bore, shaped, made aware,
  Gave, once, her flowers to love, her ways to roam,
A body of England's, breathing English air,
  Washed by the rivers, blest by suns of home.

And think, this heart, all evil shed away,
  A pulse in the eternal mind, no less
  Gives somewhere back the thoughts by England given;
Her sights and sounds; dreams happy as her day;
  And laughter, learnt of friends; and gentleness,
  In hearts at peace, under an English heaven.

Having grown up in a world were war is only in the movies or on the news, we modern readers may not quite understand the true theme of this poem. Is the speaker being sarcastic? Can he really mean what he says about willing to die for his country? The general topic is war, but a closer reading reveals actual theme, that of patriotism or more precisely, "To fight, nay even to die, in a war is a man's patriotic duty to preserve the pristine beauty of one's homeland." World War I was the first war to sweep over much of the world. It was so vicious and destructive that the old heroic ideal of a "gentleman" soldier as a worthy occupation became scarred and transformed the world's perspective of what war is. Brooke was a "pro" war poet, writing poems of inspiration at the outbreak of World War I, not knowing that it would take his own life, but also change the way wars are fought. "If I should die, think only this of me: / That there's some corner of a foreign field / That is for ever England." To show his own patriotism, Brooke enlisted in the British Navy. He didn't see much fighting but was wounded, and died a year later from blood poisoning coming from that same wound. Though his words were highly optimistic, war claimed him, as it claimed his "Soldier," an honor for anyone who wishes to preserve their way of life in the land of their fathers. However, Brooke's early death created a stir with the English public who saw him as a tragic symbol of the deadly war machine. His positive theme became lost in the wake of destruction.

Let's look at another common abstract theme: death, as found in Emily Dickinson's "Because I Could Not Stop for Death"

> Because I could not stop for Death—
> He kindly stopped for me—
> The Carriage[1] held but just Ourselves—
> And Immortality.
>
> We slowly drove—He knew no haste
> And I had put away
> My labor and my leisure too,
> For His Civility—
>
> We passed the School, where Children strove
> At Recess—in the Ring—
> We passed the Fields of Gazing Grain—
> We passed the Setting Sun—
>
> Or rather—He passed Us—
> The Dews drew quivering and chill—
> For only Gossamer,[2] my Gown—
> My Tippet[3]—only Tulle[4]—

---

1 Carriage: hearse

2 Gossamer: *n.* a thin, lightweight material

3 Tippet: *n.* scarf

4 Tulle: a thin, silk material woven into a net

We paused before a House that seemed
A Swelling of the Ground—
The Roof was scarcely visible—
The Cornice[5]—in the Ground—

Since then—'tis Centuries—and yet
Feels shorter than the Day
I first surmised the Horses' Heads
Were toward Eternity—

This poem actually shows us the speaker's trepidation with death, yet there is a beauty to it that we normally do not associate with death and funerals. The first stanza explains that the speaker did not want to die, but she has; she uses a carriage as a metaphor for death that carries her away. The journey is slow, and she can only observe. She feels like she is moving, but it is life that is actually moving on; this is the first time in her "life" she has ever had time to just sit and observe, for death makes time for all. The fourth stanza describes the death shroud she is dressed in (her gossamer gown), and the fifth stanza describes the house that is "a swelling of the ground," the tomb where she will live for eternity. The sixth stanza refers to the "Horses' Heads," which are the horses bearing her in her carriage of death, as pointing towards eternity, which is her destination. Here, in death, time has no meaning, and centuries feel like minutes. Though the speaker is dead, there is no fear in her words, only peace.

The abstract theme of this poem, of course is death, but what of the actual theme? It can be summed up as thus: "Death, though it comes to all, is not to be feared, but expected as a great journey into the unknown." If we can read a poem and pinpoint the theme, our understanding of what it is truly about will grow from that point on.

5 Cornice: *n.* a molding of stone that surrounds the roof of a building

ARS POETICA

Archibald Macleish 1892-1982

A poem should be palpable[1] and mute
As a globed fruit,

Dumb
As old medallions to the thumb

Silent as the sleeve-worn stone
Of casement[2] ledges where the moss has grown—

A poem should be wordless
As the flight of birds

A poem should be motionless in time
As the moon climbs,

Leaving, as the moon releases
Twig by twig the night-entangled trees,

Leaving, as the moon behind the winter leaves.
Memory by memory the mind—

A poem should be motionless in time
As the moon climbs.

A poem should be equal to:
Not true.

1 palpable: *adj.* easily felt by the five senses
2 casement: *n.* a window that opens outward on hinges

For all the history of grief
An empty doorway and a maple leaf.

For love
The leaning grasses and two lights above the sea—

A poem should not mean
But be.

ON THE LATE MASSACRE IN PIEDMONT

John Milton 1608-1674

Avenge O Lord thy slaughtered Saints, whose bones
Lie scattered on the Alpine mountains cold,
Even them who kept thy truth so pure of old
When all our Fathers worshiped Stocks[1] and Stones,
Forget not: in thy book[2] record their groans
Who were thy Sheep and in their ancient Fold[3]
Slain by the bloody Piemontese[4] that rolled
Mother with Infant down the Rocks. Their moans
The Vales redoubled[5] to the Hills, and they
To Heaven. Their martyred blood and ashes sow
O're all th' Italian fields where still doth sway
The triple Tyrant:[6] that from these may grow
A hundred-fold, who having learnt thy way
Early may fly the Babylonian woe.

1 Stock: *n.* wood; especially a wooden idol in this poem

2 thy book: The Book of Life; a record that God keeps of all names of his creations

3 Fold: *n.* literally a meaning a flock of sheep; here symbolically meaning members of a church

4 Piedmontese: the Waldensians, who lived in Piedmont, Italy, slaughtered by the Catholic Church

5 redouble: *v.* echo

6 the triple tyrant: The Pope, who wears a triple crown on his Papal Tiara; no longer worn today

THERE WILL COME SOFT RAINS

Sara Teasdale 1884-1933

There will come soft rains and the smell of the ground,
And swallows circling with their shimmering sound;

And frogs in the pools singing at night,
And wild plum-trees in tremulous[1] white;

Robins will wear their feathery fire
Whistling their whims on a low fence-wire;

And not one will know of the war, not one
Will care at last when it is done.

Not one would mind, neither bird nor tree
If mankind perished utterly;

And Spring herself, when she woke at dawn,
Would scarcely know that we were gone.

1 tremulous: *adj.* quivering or shaking

THE CONVERGENCE OF THE TWAIN[1]

Thomas Hardy 1840-1928

Lines on the Loss of the "Titanic"

I

In a solitude of the sea
Deep from human vanity,
And the Pride of Life that planned her,[2] stilly couches[3] she.

II

Steel chambers, late the pyres[4]
Of her salamandrine[5] fires,
Cold currents thrid,[6] and turn to rhythmic tidal lyres.

III

Over the mirrors meant
To glass the opulent
The sea-worm crawls-grotesque, slimed, dumb, indifferent.

IV

Jewels in joy designed
To ravish the sensuous mind
Lie lightless, all their sparkles bleared and black and blind.

---

1 twain: *adj.* two

2 her: the *Titanic*, a luxury sea-liner that sank after an iceberg tore open the hull on April 15, 1912, killing 1,500 of 2,200 passengers

3 couch: *v.* to lie at rest

4 pyre: *n.* a pile of wood for burning, especially for cremation

5 salamandrine: *adj.* from salamander, a mythical lizard that could live in fire

6 thrid: *v.* thread

V

Dim moon-eyed fishes near
Gaze at the gilded gear
And query: "What does this vaingloriousness[7] down here?"…

VI

Well: while was fashioning
This creature of cleaving wing,
The Immanent Will[8] that stirs and urges everything

VII

Prepared a sinister mate
For her — so gaily great —
A Shape of Ice,[9] for the time far and dissociate.[10]

VIII

And as the smart ship grew
In stature, grace, and hue,
In shadowy silent distance grew the Iceberg too.

IX

Alien they seemed to be:
No mortal eye could see
The intimate welding of their later history,

X

Or sign that they were bent
By paths coincident

---

7 vaingloriousness: *adj.* excessive pride over one's own achievements
8 Immanent Will: God
9 Shape of Ice: the iceberg that sunk the *Titanic*
10 dissociate: *v.* separate

On being anon[11] twin halves of one august[12] event,

XI

Till the Spinner of the Years[13]
Said "Now!" And each one hears,
And consummation comes, and jars two hemispheres.

11 anon: *adv.* old form meaning 'once'
12 august: *adj.* inspiring reverence
13 Spinner of the Years: God

SONNET ON CHILLON[1]

Lord George Gordon Byron 1788-1824

Eternal spirit of the chainless mind!
Brightest in dungeons, Liberty! thou art,
For there thy habitation is the heart,
The heart which love of thee alone can bind;

And when thy sons to fetters[2] are consigned[3]
To fetters, and the damp vault's dayless gloom,
Their country conquers with their martyrdom,
And Freedom's fame finds wings on every wind.

Chillon! thy prison is a holy place,
And thy sad floor an altar, for 'twas trod,
Until his very steps have left a trace

Worn, as if thy cold pavement were a sod,
By Bonnivard![4] — May none those marks efface![5]
For they appeal from tyranny to God.

---

1 Chillon: a castle located on the shore of Lake Geneva, Switzerland that once held Francois Bonnivard

2 fetter: *n.* a chain fastened to the feet

3 consign: *v.* to give over the care of one person or thing to another

4 Bonnivard: Francois Bonnivard (1496-1570), the Genovois monk imprisoned in Chillon from 1532 to 1536. At a young age, Francois opposed Charles III, the Duke of Savoy, from taking control of Geneva. For his rebellious efforts, Bonnivard was imprisoned in Chillon for three years.

5 efface: *v.* to erase

STOPPING BY THE WOODS ON A SNOWY EVENING

Robert Frost 1874-1963

Whose woods these are I think I know.
His house is in the village, though;
He will not see me stopping here
To watch his woods fill up with snow.

My little horse must think it queer
To stop without a farmhouse near
Between the woods and frozen lake
The darkest evening of the year.

He gives his harness bells a shake
To ask if there is some mistake.
The only other sound's the sweep
Of easy wind and downy flake.

The woods are lovely, dark, and deep,
But I have promises to keep,
And miles to go before I sleep,
And miles to go before I sleep.

ELEMENT ***THREE:***

FIGURES OF SPEECH

Introduction to Element *Three*: Figures of Speech

Language is full of figurative language. When a friend says, "I didn't mean to say that. It was a slip of the tongue," he doesn't literally mean his tongue has slipped in his mouth, for how is that possible? We understand that he has said something by accident. The English language is full of such figurative language, or figures of speech, and poetry exercises it the best. There are over 250 different forms of figures of speech. We will focus on the four basic and most popular forms.

The first form is the **metaphor** where one object is identified with another, and the first object takes on the characteristics of the second. If a picture is worth a thousand words, so then is a metaphor. I could say that John is a tiger. Do I mean that there is a tiger named John? Not likely. What I mean is that John takes on the characteristics of a tiger. Instead of going through a shopping list of attributes about John's temperamental and feisty nature, I can just paint a picture in the mind using a metaphor. We now know that when we are around John, we should be careful of his temper and anger, lest he lashes out. A vivid example of metaphor is found in Andrew Marvell's "To His Coy Mistress," where he writes, "Time's winged chariot hurrying near." Now we know that time does not ride a chariot nor do chariots fly. Thus, the metaphor conjures images of the god Apollo riding his chariot through the heavens, while creating the image of time being fast and always on the move, being immortal.

Traditionally, metaphors were the staple of poets, though they are used much more conservatively in modern times. While most poets restrict metaphors to single instances, classical poets often employed the extended metaphor where the metaphorical symbol is developed beyond the single word. For example, Walt Whitman's "O Captain!

My Captain!" is a fitting eulogy written after the assassination of Abraham Lincoln.

> O Captain! my Captain, our fearful trip is done,
> The ship has weathered every rack, the prize we sought is won,
> The port is near, the bells I hear, the people all exulting,
> While follow eyes the steady keel, the vessel grim and daring;
>   But O heart! heart! heart!
>   O the bleeding drips of red,
>   Where on the deck my Captain lies,
>   Fallen cold and dead.

Utilizing **apostrophe**, a figure of speech where the speaker directly speaks to someone not present, Whitman gives adoration to Lincoln, whose death shocked the nation. Whitman spoke about how he had a dream of a ship under full sail entering the harbor the night before Lincoln was shot. Whitman couples the ship entering port imagery with metaphors of President Lincoln as the captain of the ship, which represents the newly won Union of the American states. Lincoln, as the captain, has survived the tumultuous storm (The Civil War) that almost destroyed his vessel (America). Just as he nears the port (the end of the war), he is received as a hero; but, to the dismay of those waiting, he has "fallen cold and dead" on the deck of his ship.

Metaphor is also beautifully woven in William Butler Yeats' "A Coat," which explores the idea of art as a song he has created.

> I made my song a coat
> Covered with embroideries
> Out of old mythologies
> From heel to throat;
> But the fools caught it,
> Wore it in the world's eyes
> As though they'd wrought[1] it.
> Song, let them take it,
> For there's more enterprise
> In walking naked.

---

1 wrought: *v.* made

Yeats uses the metaphor that his creation fits him as a coat and the embroidery that makes it beautiful has been crafted out of things from his past that he can readily identify with. However, when others come along and take his coat, which he has put a lot of time and effort into so that it looks appealing; they wear it and show it off as if they were special. This is similar to academics who sit around all day quoting their favorite poets, sounding important and learned, but have done nothing creative themselves. It is even similar to when we sing famous songs of our favorite pop artists, showing our prowess with a song that is, in fact, not our own. We have created nothing, and yet many envy our skill at wearing another's beautiful coat. Yeats says, however, to let these people have the coat. It actually shows their own uncreativeness, while he would rather go naked, for there is more complication and risk in the very act of not creating. Such an act would eventually equal out where all then would have to go naked, having no skill to make their own coat, yet the artist still remains an artist, while everyone else is just naked!

Another type of figure of speech is related to the metaphor—**personification**, or giving human characteristics to animals, inanimate objects, or natural occurrences. Take, for example, John Donne's profound "Holy Sonnet 10."

> Death be not proud, though some have called thee
> Mighty and dreadful, for thou are not so;
> For those whom thou thinkst, thou does overthrow
> Die not, poor death, nor yet canst thou kill me.
> From rest and sleep, which but they pictures be,
> Much pleasure—then from thee much more must flow,
> And soonest our best men with thee do go,
> Rest of their bones, and soul's delivery.
> Thou art slave to fate, chance, kings, and desperate men,
> And dost with poison, war, and sickness dwell,
> And poppy or charms can make us sleep as well,
> And better then thy stroke; why swellst thou then?
> One short sleep past, we wake eternally
> And death shall be no more; Death, thou shalt die.

Here, Death is personified as a being a real person. By doing so, the poet can tap into a vast vault of symbolism, knowing the reader will understand the figurative language being used. In literature, Death is often a figure to be feared, and, as in John Milton's *Paradise Lost*, Death is even greater than Satan while having the power to even harm him. Donne only scoffs at that image. His sonnet explains the absolute powerlessness Death actually has over us. We all die, but it is a gate to a greater place. This horrible apparition that is Death is merely a slave of "fate, chance, kings, and desperate men" who are the ones that actually decide who will live or die, and not Death himself. Death's only companions, it turns out, are "poison, war, and sickness," but we can imitate death with certain drugs (the poppy) and charms (hypnotism), so what is so special about what Death does? While we go on to live for eternity through Christ's resurrection, Death will eventually end, and he, not us, shall die. Now try writing a poem on such a topic without invoking figures of speech. It would be nearly impossible.

A third common type of figure of speech is the **simile**. Where a metaphor simply states one idea for another, a simile uses comparison through the words *like* or *as*. To make a distinction between a metaphor and a simile, let's look at the first two lines of "A Red, Red Rose" by Robert Burns. "O my luve's like a red, red rose / That's newly sprung in June." This is a simile where his love becomes like a red rose; it is an approximation. It is like saying in a mathematical formula Love ~ Red Rose. If the poet had wanted to use metaphor, he would have phrased it this way: "O my love is a red, red rose." As a metaphor, his love takes on the characteristics of the red rose; they are both equal in meaning. Thus, the associations that the sentence brings to the meaning are broader than the simile. The mathematical formula would be Love = Red Rose. The simile only stipulates that his love is like a red rose, so the comparison is limited in its approximation. The metaphor can literally have every single quality that a red rose may possess, including all the connotations. With this understanding we can understand how far the poet wants us to take the symbolism used. With similes, we are restricted; with metaphors, we are freer in our interpretations.

Do not confuse the **hyperbole**, another figure of speech, with a simile. Hyperboles are often written as similes, as in "he is as tall as a mountain," except the only function this statement has is to exaggerate the concept of how tall he is. A hyperbole, Greek for "excess," is often used poetically as an extreme form of exaggeration, where poets wish to highlight atypical and expressive imagery. Sylvia Plath exercises hyperbole in "Daddy" to express how much influence she feels her father has held over her. "Daddy, I have to kill you. / You died before I had time — / Marble-heavy, a bag full of gold, / Ghastly statue with one gray toe / Big as a Frisco seal / And a head in the freakish Atlantic." Here Plath expresses both metaphor and hyperbole to detail her own feeling about her father's influence over her as being so overwhelming and grand that his control is a colossal statue stretched from the Atlantic Ocean in the west all the way to San Fransico (Frisco) in the east. The toe of this metaphorical statue is the size of a San Francisco seal that is well known for its large size, which is expressed as a hyperbole.

Another hyperbole that does not use comparison is just gross exaggeration, as found in "The Concord Hymn" by Ralph Waldo Emerson. "Here once the embattled farmers stood; / And fired the shot heard round the world." Written in commemoration of the first battle of the American Revolution, we can see that the revolutionaries first shot that started the war, could not literally be heard around the world, but the idea that the effect of this shot, would have repercussions that would be felt around the world.

DAFFODILS

William Wordsworth 1770 - 1850

I wandered lonely as a cloud
That floats on high o'er vales and hills,
When all at once I saw a crowd,
A host, of golden daffodils;
Beside the lake, beneath the trees,
Fluttering and dancing in the breeze.

Continuous as the stars that shine
And twinkle on the milky way,
They stretched in never-ending line
Along the margin of a bay:
Ten thousand saw I at a glance,
Tossing their heads in sprightly dance.

The waves beside them danced; but they
Out-did the sparkling waves in glee:
A poet could not but be gay,
In such a jocund[1] company:
I gazed — and gazed — but little thought
What wealth the show to me had brought:

For oft, when on my couch I lie
In vacant or in pensive mood,
They flash upon that inward eye
Which is the bliss of solitude;
And then my heart with pleasure fills,
And dances with the daffodils.

1 jocund: *adj.* cheerful

THE ROAD NOT TAKEN

Robert Frost 1874-1963

Two roads diverged in a yellow wood,
And sorry I could not travel both
And be one traveler, long I stood
And looked down one as far as I could
To where it bent in the undergrowth;

Then took the other, as just as fair,
And having perhaps the better claim,
Because it was grassy and wanted wear;
Though as for that the passing there
Had worn them really about the same,

And both that morning equally lay
In leaves no step had trodden black.
Oh, I kept the first for another day!
Yet knowing how way leads on to way,
I doubted if I should ever come back.

I shall be telling this with a sigh
Somewhere ages and ages hence:
Two roads diverged in a wood, and I—
I took the one less traveled by,
And that has made all the difference.

SONNET 19

William Shakespeare 1564-1616

Devouring Time, blunt thou the lion's paws,
And make the earth devour her own sweet brood;
Pluck the keen[1] teeth from the fierce tiger's jaws,
And burn the long-lived phoenix[2] in her blood;
Make glad and sorry seasons as thou fleets,[3]
And do whate'er thou wilt, swift-footed Time,
To the wide world and all her fading sweets;
But I forbid thee one most heinous crime:
O, carve not with thy hours my love's fair brow,
Nor draw no lines there with thine[4] antique pen;
Him in thy[5] course untainted do allow
For beauty's pattern to succeeding men.
    Yet, do thy worst, old Time: despite thy wrong,
    My love shall in my verse ever live young.

---

1 keen: *adj.* razor sharp

2 phoenix: *n.* a mythical bird that lives hundreds of years only to die by self-combusting and rising out of its ashes to start a fresh cycle

3 fleet: *v.* to fly

4 thine: (pro) old form meaning 'your'

5 thy: (pro) old form meaning 'your'; 'thine' comes before vowels while 'thy' comes before consonants

TO HIS COY[1] MISTRESS

Andrew Marvell 1621-1678

Had we but world enough, and time,
This coyness, lady, were no crime.
We would sit down, and think which way
To walk, and pass our long love's day.
Thou by the Indian Ganges'[2] side
Shouldst rubies find; I by the tide
Of Humber[3] would complain.[4] I would
Love you ten years before the Flood,[5]
And you should, if you please, refuse
Till the conversion of the Jews.[6]
My vegetable love should grow
Vaster than empires, and more slow;
An hundred years should go to praise
Thine eyes, and on thy forehead gaze;
Two hundred to adore each breast,
But thirty thousand to the rest;
An age at least to every part,
And the last age should show your heart.
For, lady, you deserve this state,
Nor would I love at lower rate.
But at my back I always hear

1 coy: *adj.* shy or modest

2 Ganges: a major river flowing out of the Himalayas into India; considered sacred

3 Humber: a small muddy river in Trent, England that is the complete opposite of what the Ganges would be

4 complain: *v.* poetic form meaning "moaning plaintive poems of love"

5 the Flood: the great Biblical Flood in the time of Noah that encompassed the whole earth

6 conversion of the Jews: a popular Christian motif having the Jews convert just before the Last Judgment of God

Time's wingéd chariot hurrying near;
And yonder[7] all before us lie
Deserts of vast eternity.
Thy beauty shall no more be found,
Nor, in thy marble vault shall sound
My echoing song; then worms shall try
That long-preserved virginity,
And your quaint honor turn to dust,
And into ashes all my lust:
The grave's a fine and private place,
But none, I think, do there embrace.
Now therefore, while the youthful hue[8]
Sits on thy skin like morning dew,
And while thy willing soul transpires[9]
At every pore with instant fires,[10]
Now let us sport us while we may,
And now, like amorous[11] birds of prey,
Rather at once our time devour
Than languish in his slow-chapped[12] power.
Let us roll all our strength and all
Our sweetness up into one ball,
And tear our pleasures with rough strife[13]
Thorough[14] the iron gates of life.
Thus, though we cannot make our sun
Stand still, yet we will make him run.

7 yonder: *adj.* over there

8 hue: *n.* color

9 transpire: *v.* to give off or emit

10 instant fires: immediate passion

11 amorous: *adj.* showing love

12 slow-chapped: also meaning 'slow-jawed'; a metaphor for time slowly eating the world and the people

13 strife: *n.* struggle

14 thorough: *adj.* old form meaning 'through'

FOG

Carl Sandburg 1878-1967

The fog comes
on little cat feet.

It sits looking
over harbor and city
on silent haunches
and then moves on.

AH, SUNFLOWER

William Blake 1757-1827

Ah, sunflower, weary of time,
Who countest[1] the steps of the sun,
Seeking after that sweet golden clime
Where the traveler's journey is done:

Where the Youth pined away with desire,
And the pale virgin shrouded in snow
Arise from their graves, and aspire
Where my Sunflower wishes to go.

1 countest: *v.* old form meaning 'counts'

ELEMENT *FOUR*: DICTION

Introduction to Element *Four*: Diction

Poetry is like a feast of words. If we are to attend a banquet, how boring it would be to feast upon the same old dish and flavor time and again. A feast means that we satiate ourselves on a variety of flavors and textures. Poets are the same as chefs at a banquet. They test, combine, and struggle over each and every word written on the page. Nothing gets past their scrutiny. In order to enjoy and experience the craft of the poet, we must slow down and savor the language the poet has so tirelessly written for our pleasure. Would we sit down at a banquet and quickly eat the food? Or would we simply sit and enjoy the menagerie of flavors the chefs had cooked for us? Poetry is the same. Giving it patience, we will be rewarded with some of the best crafted language in history.

Diction has traditionally been recognized as language with a natural poetic excellence that stands out from the common usage. Some common words deemed poetical are "betwixt" for "between" and "art" for "are," and are only found in poems. Though this was the case before the 19th century, the romantic poets with Wordsworth at the head wanted to bridge the gap "betwixt" this so called poetic style of speech and everyday spoken language, which lead to poetic diction becoming more "down to earth" or regular in execution. In contemporary poetry, such archaic style of diction is used more or less for an ironic effect, affording the poet a wider template of language.

In reading poetry, we not only need to know the meaning of the words but also what they imply. Words contain both denotations and connotations. The **denotation** is the meaning found in the dictionary. It is rather dull on its own, rather like all the separate ingredients in the kitchen, not very appetizing. If I say the word "wine," the denotation is "fermented juice of grapes." That is rather a dull way of looking at the word. However, the **connotation**, or the emotional idea or attitude of the word, is more romantic since wine is used during romantic candlelit dinners. It also conjures up religious images of the blood of Christ as hinted at during the Last Supper and used in Catholic mass. Thus, the connotation carries the most significance in the reading of words. When all the ingredients or words are combined, then the mundane denotations give way to a feast of connotations, which are what you need to focus on more in reading poetry.

Since poets do not write anything except those words that work best for the poem, the reader must understand how these words add to feelings, and what is implied in the words instead of what is meant. Thus, we must get into the habit of reading for both the denotation and connotation of the words. Let's examine Lord Alfred Tennyson's "The Eagle":

> He clasps the crag with crooked hands;
> Close to the sun in lonely lands,
> Ringed with the azure world, he stands.
> The wrinkled sea beneath him crawls;
> He watches from his mountain walls,
> And like a thunderbolt he falls.

First of all, as astute readers, we need to look at the word "hands." Why does the speaker use a human word for a bird? Why not use "talons"? If we read only the denotation, then the meaning can be confusing. However, what the connotation conjures in our minds is quite different. Lord Tennyson is personifying the regal creature and giving it a more human characteristic; thus, what happens to the eagle has direct consequences to the human race as well. This is further accentuated by starting the poem with the masculine/human form of "he".

The use of the nouns in the poem are rather simplistic: "hands", "lands", "world", "sea", and "walls." However, what creates concrete imagery are the adjectives next to these nouns. "Crooked" could easily be replaced by "bent" or "curved." However the use of "crooked" brings to mind several acceptable denotations. According to the *Oxford English Dictionary*, "crooked" could mean "bent or twisted; a deformed person; dishonest or corrupt." With any of these definitions the meaning of the poem can change or transform. That is the denotation. What about the connotations?

"Crooked hands" bring to my mind malformed hands or even hands of an elderly man, perhaps the hands of a once mighty king that are bent with age. Another word that stands out is "azure." The denotation is a bright blue color; "pertaining to a sea-god; cloudless; or serene." The connotation conjures a blue world of majesty that the eagle rules over with "mountain walls" being synonymous with castle walls. How would the connotation change if it was written as "blue world"? In fact let's change the connotation of the whole poem without changing the denotation by using synonyms (of course rhyme and meter will be broken, but that will be discussed in later chapters):

> It grabs the cliff with curved claws;
> Close to the sun in lost areas,
> Enclosed in the blue sky, it stands.
> The undulating sea below moves;
> It watches from its mountain face,
> And like a rock it plummets.

The poem keeps the denotative meaning of the poem accurately; however, ignoring the rhyme and meter change, the connotation of the poet is not only completely transformed, it further becomes base and common.

Finally, in the last stanza are the words "thunderbolt" and "falls." Both words are incongruent. A thunderbolt connotes a form of power, the influence of the gods, stately. However, "falls" connotes a form of inanimation. Not only does it conjure images of a rock falling, but also the Biblical Fall, as a person of high stature reduced to nothing. We could easily read it as an eagle launching from its perch on the mountain ledge and is dropping like a thunderbolt down to some unsuspecting prey below. However, if we choose to take all the connotations in the poem together—the personification, the royalty of the bird's domain, the mountainous, fortress like walls of its perch—then another connotation comes to light. We could easily read it that someone has shot the poor bird and it suddenly plummets to its death, like a thunderbolt striking the earth, reminding the reader that not only the majesty of nature, but of all humanity, is frail and precariously so. Through understanding diction, the interpretation of this poem shows that nature can consume all things on a whim, but we humans can consume it quicker and more effortlessly.

LONDON

William Blake 1757-1827

I wander through each chartered[1] street,
Near where the chartered Thames[2] does flow,
And mark in every face I meet,
Marks of weakness, marks of woe.

In every cry of every Man,
In every Infant's cry of fear,
In every voice, in every ban,
The mind-forged manacles[3] I hear.

How the Chimney-sweeper's cry
Every blackening Church appalls;[4]
And the hapless[5] Soldier's sigh
Runs in blood down Palace walls.

But most, through midnight streets I hear
How the youthful Harlot's[6] curse
Blasts the new born Infant's tear,
And blights with plagues the Marriage hearse.

1 chartered: *adj.* a written form granting ownership; owned
2 Thames: the main river that flows through London, England
3 manacle: *n.* handcuff
4 appall: *v.* to fill with dread
5 hapless: *adj.* unlucky
6 harlot: *n.* a prostitute

CARGOES

John Masefield 1878-1967

Quinquireme[1] of Nineveh[2] from distant Ophir[3],
Rowing home to haven in sunny Palestine[4],
With a cargo of ivory,
And apes and peacocks,
Sandalwood, cedarwood, and sweet white wine.

Stately Spanish galleon coming from the Isthmus[5],
Dipping through the Tropics by the palm-green shores,
With a cargo of diamonds,
Emeralds, amethysts,
Topazes, and cinnamon, and gold moidores[6].

Dirty British coaster[7] with a salt-caked smoke-stack,
Butting through the Channel in the mad March days,
With a cargo of Tyne[8] coal,
Road-rails, pig-lead,[9]
Firewood, iron-ware, and cheap tin trays.

1 quinquireme: *n.* an ancient cargo ship that had five levels of oars to move the ship
2 Nineveh: ancient Assyrian capital; ruins now located in Northern Iraq
3 Ophir: ancient city of wealth mentioned in the Old Testament
4 Palestine: The eastern shores of the Mediterranean occupied by Israel, Jordan, and Egypt
5 Isthmus: probably the Isthmus of Suez in Egypt that connect the Mediterranean Sea with the Red Sea
6 moidore: *n.* a Portuguese gold coin
7 coaster: *n.* a ship that trades along the coast
8 Tyne: from the river located in NE England
9 pig-lead: *n.* lead molded as pigs to increase sales value

ON FIRST LOOKING INTO CHAPMAN'S HOMER[1]

John Keats 1795-1821

Much have I travelled in the realms of gold,
And many goodly states and kingdoms seen;
Round many western islands have I been
Which bards in fealty to Apollo[2] hold.
Oft of one wide expanse had I been told
That deep-browed Homer[3] ruled as his demesne;[4]
Yet did I never breathe its pure serene
Till I heard Chapman speak out loud and bold:
Then felt I like some watcher of the skies
When a new planet[5] swims into his ken;[6]
Or like stout Cortez[7] when with eagle eyes
He stared at the Pacific — and all his men
Looked at each other with a wild surmise —
Silent, upon a peak in Darien.[8]

1 Chapman's Homer: George Chapman (1559-1634), a classical scholar, who first translated both Homer's *Iliad* and *Odyssey* into English.

2 Apollo: The Greek and Roman god of poetry

3 Homer: 9th century B.C. Greek poet of the *Iliad* and *Odyssey*

4 demesne: *n.* a district or region

5 new planet: Neptune

6 ken: *n.* knowledge

7 Cortez: Hernan Cortez (1485-1547), a Spanish explorer; however, was not the first to see the Pacific; credit is given to a less famous Spanish explorer Balboa

8 Darien: a mountain in eastern Panama, Central America

IT IS A BEAUTEOUS EVENING

William Wordsworth 1770-1850

It is a beauteous evening, calm and free,
The holy time is quiet as a Nun
Breathless with adoration; the broad sun
Is sinking down in its tranquility;
The gentleness of heavens broods o'er the Sea:
Listen! the mighty Being[1] is awake,
And doth with his eternal motion make
A sound like thunder — everlastingly.
Dear Child! dear Girl! that walkest with me here,
If thou appear untouched by solemn thought,
Thy nature is not therefore less divine:
Thou liest in Abraham's bosom[2] all the year,
And worship'st at the Temple's inner shrine,
God being with thee when we know it not.

1 mighty Being: God
2 Abraham's bosom: Heaven

MINIVER CHEEVY

Edwin Arlington Robinson 1869-1935

Miniver Cheevy, child of scorn,
Grew lean while he assailed the seasons
He wept that he was ever born,
And he had reasons.

Miniver loved the days of old
When swords were bright and steeds were prancing;
The vision of a warrior bold
Would send him dancing.

Miniver sighed for what was not,
And dreamed, and rested from his labors;
He dreamed of Thebes[1] and Camelot,[2]
And Priam's[3] neighbors.

Miniver mourned the ripe renown
That made so many a name so fragrant;
He mourned Romance, now on the town,
And Art, a vagrant.

Miniver loved the Medici,[4]
Albeit he had never seen one;
He would have sinned incessantly

1 Thebes: ancient city in Greece that had importance in Greek myth
2 Camelot: the mythical castle of King Arthur
3 Priam: King of Troy as mentioned in Greek myth; important figure in the Trojan War
4 the Medici: a rich family of aristocratic Italian bankers that held great influence from the 15th to the 17th century

Could he have been one.

Miniver cursed the commonplace
And eyed a khaki suit[5] with loathing:
He missed the medieval grace
Of iron clothing.

Miniver scorned the gold he sought,
But sore annoyed was he without it;
Miniver thought, and thought, and thought,
And thought about it.

Miniver Cheevy, born too late,
Scratched his head and kept on thinking;
Miniver coughed, and called it fate,
And kept on drinking.

5 khaki suit: *n.* a military uniform

JABBERWOCKY

Lewis Carroll 1832-1893

Twas *brillig*, and the *slithy toves*
Did *gyre* and *gimble* in the *wabe*;
All *mimsy* were the *borogoves*,
And the *mome raths outgrabe*.

"Beware the *Jabberwock*, my son!
The jaws that bite, the claws that catch!
Beware the *Jubjub* bird, and shun
The *frumious Bandersnatch*!"

He took his *vorpal* sword in hand:
Long time the *manxome* foe he sought—
So rested he by the *Tumtum* tree,
And stood awhile in thought.

And as in *uffish* thought he stood,
The *Jabberwock*, with eyes of flame,
Came *whiffling* through the *tulgey* wood,
And burbled[1] as it came!

One, two! One, two! and through and through
The *vorpal* blade went *snicker-snack*!
He left it dead, and with its head
He went galumphing[2] back.

1 burble: *v.* to make a bubbling sound
2 galumph: *v.* to gallop; a word invented by Carroll that is now part of the English lexicon

"And hast thou slain the *Jabberwock*?
Come to my arms, my beamish boy!
O *frabjous* day! *Callooh*! *Callay*!"
He chortled[3] in his joy.

'Twas *brillig*, and the *slithy toves*
Did *gyre* and *gimble* in the *wabe*;
All *mimsy* were the *borogoves*,
And the *mome raths outgrabe*.

3 chortle: *v*. a rough laugh; another word invented by Carroll that is now part of the English lexicon

A VALEDICTION: FORBIDDING MOURNING[1]

John Donne 1572-1631

As virtuous men pass mildly away,
    And whisper to their souls to go,
Whilst some of their sad friends do say,
    "Now his breath goes,[2]" and some say, "No."

So let us melt, and make no noise,
    No tear-floods, nor sigh-tempests move;
'Twere profanation[3] of our joys
    To tell the laity[4] our love.

Moving of th' earth brings harms and fears;
    Men reckon what it did, and meant;
But trepidation of the spheres,[5]
    Though greater far, is innocent.

Dull sublunary[6] lovers' love
    —Whose soul is sense—cannot admit
Of absence, 'cause it doth remove
    The thing which elemented[7] it.

1 Donne wrote this poem to his wife when he travelled to Europe and felt that something bad would happen to her. Something bad did happen: she gave birth to a stillborn child.

2 Now his breath goes: dies

3 profanation: *n.* defilement

4 laity: *n.* a congregation of worshippers in a church

5 trepidation of the spheres: a reference to the then misunderstanding of the sky. Astronomers thought everything to move in perfect circular orbits. When this did not happen, it was called the shaking of the spheres. This was considered natural. The earth wobbling on its axis accounts for these irregularities.

6 sublunary: *adj.* beneath the moon; sublunary lovers are earth bound and subject to the change experienced on earth

But we by a love so much refined,
    That ourselves know not what it is,
Inter-assurèd[8] of the mind,
    Care less, eyes, lips and hands to miss.

Our two souls therefore, which are one,
    Though I must go, endure not yet
A breach, but an expansion,
    Like gold to aery[9] thinness beat.

If they be two, they are two so
    As stiff twin compasses[10] are two;
Thy soul, the fixed foot,[11] makes no show
    To move, but doth, if th' other do.

And though it in the centre sit,
    Yet, when the other[12] far doth roam,
It leans, and hearkens after it,
    And grows erect, as that comes home.

Such wilt thou be to me, who must,
    Like th' other foot, obliquely run;
Thy firmness makes my circle just,
    And makes me end where I begun.

---

7 elemented: *v.* old form meaning 'created'
8 interassured: *v.* to know for sure
9 aery: *adj.* composed of air
10 compass: *n.* a drawing instrument that is used to draw a perfect circle
11 fixed foot: the pointed end of the compass that serves as the anchor
12 the other: the other end of the compass that moves around the center

HOW DO I LOVE THEE

Elizabeth Browning 1806-1861

How do I love thee? Let me count the ways.
I love thee to the depth and breadth and height
My soul can reach, when feeling out of sight
For the ends of being and ideal grace.
I love thee to the level of every day's
Most quiet need, by sun and candle-light.
I love thee freely, as men strive for right.
I love thee purely, as they turn from praise.
I love thee with the passion put to use
In my old griefs, and with my childhood's faith.
I love thee with a love I seemed to lose
With my lost saints. I love thee with the breath,
Smiles, tears, of all my life; and, if God choose,
I shall but love thee better after death.

ELEMENT *FIVE*:
IRONY AND PARADOX

Introduction to Element *Five*: IRONY AND PARADOX

Poetry like art beautifies the world around us: paintings of beautiful landscapes, the Mona Lisa smile, a poem about a field of daffodils, and the well chiseled David to name a few. Any type of art that attempts to show the uglier side of people or society is often not popular; it exists for sure, but how many people have a painting of a garbage heap hanging in their living room? Modern poets are actually known for their portrayal of the everyday, such as T. S. Eliot's "The Winter Evening Settles Down," which is a beautifully written poem about the ugliness of a modern London street. It could be argued that Eliot's poem is not that ugly of a topic; it is something any urban dweller sees on a daily basis and that is the point. But how many mainstream poems are there on rape, abortion, murder, suicide, and other unsavory topics? Outside of avant-garde publications, these poems do not have an audience, but such topics do, in fact, exist in many poems throughout history; the passive reader just may not notice them at first. Poets are usually the first to bring to press the unsavory or neglected parts of society to light, and they can do it successfully through the use of both irony and paradox.

Irony is manipulating language to express the opposite meaning written often in a humorous fashion. Irony is the perfect form to deal with concepts or ideas that society may be uncomfortable hearing or dealing with. Irony is successful as a poetic element because it **is** the truth no matter how unwelcome the idea. When reading irony, a perceptive reader may find it humorous or disturbing, depending on the goal of the poet. The poem may push a wedge between what appears to be the truth and the reality of the truth. For example, in Samuel Taylor Coleridge's "Rhyme of the Ancient Mariner," he deftly uses irony when he writes:

Water, water, every where,
And all the boards did shrink;
Water, water, every where,
Nor any drop to drink.

The appearance of water and the reality of it are two different concepts. A sailor, who has run out of water on the high seas like the Mariner, understands this idea all too well. This is called **situational irony** that contrasts what the reader expects with what really happens. What is expected is that if water is everywhere then it should be drunk, but the situational irony is that it is ocean water, and though it looks refreshing, it cannot be imbibed.

Let's look at how irony is used in another poem. Stephen Crane deals ironically with the theme of disillusionment in "A Man Saw a Ball of Gold."

A man saw a ball of gold in the sky;
He climbed for it,
And eventually he achieved it—
It was clay.

Now this is the strange part:
When the man went to the earth
And looked again,
Lo, there was a ball of gold.
Now this is the strange part:
It was a ball of gold.
Ay, by the heavens, it was a ball of gold.

The irony is found in line four when the "ball of gold" turns out to be nothing but clay! Why is that ironic? Gold is held in high esteem. It is recognized the world over as a precious metal worth achieving, yet when we do achieve it, the ball of gold actually becomes clay. We may vote for a president that promises to change the status quo of the country only to be elected and become the status quo. The double irony of this poem, though, is that the ball of gold that we have seen as worthless clay actually is, in reality, a ball of gold. We buy items that are clearly valuable, only to find out that after paying the high price for the item, it ceases to be valuable to us; it is just another item we own.

When irony becomes more biting and critical in what is says, it has turned into **sarcasm**. Jonathan Swift was perhaps one of the best poets to use sarcasm effectively and popularly. In the poem "On Ink" Swift shows the discrepancy between our idea of what ink is and the actual power it has; "the pen is mightier than the sword" indeed.

I am jet black, as you may see,
The son of pitch[1] and gloomy night;
Yet all that know me will agree,
I'm dead except I live in light.

Sometimes in panegyric[2] high,
Like lofty Pindar,[3] I can soar,
And raise a virgin to the sky,
Or sink her to a filthy ——.

My blood this day is very sweet,
To-morrow of a bitter juice;
Like milk, 'tis cried about the street,
And so applied to different use.

Most wondrous is my magic power:
For with one color I can paint;
I'll make the devil a saint this hour,
Next make a devil of a saint.

Through distant regions I can fly,
Provide me but with paper wings;
And fairly show a reason why
There should be quarrels among kings;

1 pitch: *n.* tar
2 panegyric: *n.* a lofty praise of a person or thing; eulogy
3 Pindar: ancient Greek poet

And, after all, you'll think it odd,
When learned doctors will dispute,
That I should point the word of God,
And show where they can best confute.

Let lawyers bawl and strain their throats
'Tis I that must the lands convey,
And strip their clients to their coats;
Nay, give their very souls away.

Here we have the personification of ink speaking sarcastically to us, the reader. Swift once wrote in the Preface to *The Battle of the Books* (1704), "Satire is a sort of glass wherein beholders do generally discover everybody's face but their own." Irony and sarcasm, as a form of satire, are indeed popular because we can see the irony in the lives of others but not ourselves; thus, we keep reading. "On Ink" does this successfully. All the horrible things we write and profess with pen and ink are dumped on the "scapegoat" ink. Because ink is personified, it becomes the villain, not the person who writes with it. The sarcasm of this poem can be restated in another modern form, "Guns don't kill people, bullets do." This phrase shifts the blame from the gun that is seen as violent to something else entirely—the bullet, and yet it has an essence of truth. But what is missing is the real idea behind the quote, that being, "Guns don't kill people, people do." "On Ink" is performing a similar function, albeit 400 years earlier. By focusing on the evils that we commit in the written form, the poem allows us to force the blame onto others—lawyers, politicians, writers. We fail to see that the poem implicates us in this negative action, which is why we are drawn to it, but it does raise the issue of the damage the written word causes society without making anyone angry.

Paradox is another popular element in poems. What may at first seem contradictory starts to make sense upon a second or third reading. It is similar to irony in that they both are aware of illusion and reality, and what we read must not always be taken at face value. A common modern paradox is that we drive our car to a trendy health club, take the elevator up to the tenth floor, then get on the stair machine. To someone who is not a modern, this appears as a paradox, to the rest of us we can understand why it can be a paradox, but understand why it is so. Just running up stairs is not the main source of exercise; we want to feel connected to others by being part of a "group" or established "product." For a sense of paradox, let's look at the first stanza of John Keats's "Ode to a Nightingale."

> My heart aches, and a drowsy numbness pains
> My sense, as though of hemlock[4] I had drunk,
> Or emptied some dull opiate to the drains[5]
> One minute past, and Lethe-wards[6] had sunk:
> 'Tis not through envy of thy happy lot,
> But being too happy in thine happiness,—
> That thou, light-winged Dryad[7] of the trees,
> In some melodious plot
> Of beechen[8] green, and shadows numberless,
> Singest of summer in full-throated ease.

This first stanza introduces the nightingale as being "too happy in thine happiness." Viewing such happiness causes the speaker to feel bouts of both pain and joy. The paradox is expressed when the speaker states in the first line that his heart aches while being overcome with drowsy numbness. On first reading, we may wonder how the speaker can ache and be numb all at once. Such a paradox creates a shocking image of pain of how the speaker feels hearing the voice of a nightingale. This contradictory phrasing is known as an **oxymoron**, which lies at the center of many paradoxes. When the speaker says "drowsy numbness pains," he is speaking of a pain that is so intense that he cannot deal with it so that the pain finally numbs his senses.

4 hemlock: *n.* a poisonous drink
5 drain: *n.* meaning something that has drained away
6 Lethe-wards: towards Lethe, a mythical river in Hades where the dead drank to forget the past
7 Dryad: nymphs that live in forests
8 beechen: *adj.* of relating to a beech tree

This is how the speaker can paradoxically feel a numbness that can cause pain. We can take away from this paradox that the speaker knows he will never be like the nightingale, free from the pains of the world.

Another type of paradox is found in religious poetry, the idea that fallen, imperfect humans can somehow follow and obey an exalted, perfect God. Nobody experienced the paradox of religion more than George Herbert (1593-1633), a minister of a church who found it difficult to call a congregation of sinners to repentance while he himself was also a sinner, for ministers are human, and, therefore, sin. This paradox is wonderfully expressed in "The Collar."

I struck the board,[9] and cried, No more;
I will abroad.
What? shall I ever sigh and pine?[10]
My lines and life are free; free as the road,
Loose as the wind, as large as store.[11]
Shall I be still in suit?[12]
Have I no harvest but a thorn
To let me blood, and not restore
What I have lost with cordial[13] fruit?
Sure there was wine,
Before my sighs did dry it: there was corn
Before my tears did drown it.
Is the year only lost to me?
Have I no bays[14] to crown it?
No flowers, no garlands gay? all blasted?
All wasted?
Not so, my heart: but there is fruit,
And thou hast hands.
Recover all thy sigh-blown age
On double pleasures: leave thy cold dispute
Of what is fit, and not forsake thy cage,

9 board: *n.* table
10 pine: *v.* regret or yearn
11 store: *n.* abundance
12 suit: *adj.* asking favors
13 cordial: *adj.* life-giving
14 bay: *n.* a wreath of leaves; a laurel worn by poets

Thy rope of sands,[15]
Which petty thoughts have made, and made to thee
Good cable, to enforce and draw,
And be thy law,
While thou didst wink and wouldst not see.
Away; take heed:
I will abroad.
Call in thy deaths-head[16] there: tie up thy fears.
He that forbears
To suit and serve his need,
Deserves his load.
But as I raved and grew more fierce and wild,
At every word,
Me thought I heard one calling, *Child*:
And I replied, *My Lord.*

Here, the speaker, also a minister, strikes the board of table set with meat and fruit. It appears that he was in the midst of prayer and ends it by striking the table and says he will leave his life of ministry ("I will abroad"). He complains that God has given him nothing but misery for faithful service, a thorn instead of fruit. The corn and wine of the sacrament he sees only as temporal rewards—he has forgotten the eternal significance of these emblems. He plans on a life of pleasure before he is too old. He calls his service to God a cage and God's law as shackles. While he raves and grows "more fierce and wild," he hears the still, small voice of God call out, "Child!" He responds, "My Lord." The paradox is that a sinner by the very nature of the word is a person who is in opposition to the laws of God. Furthermore, the speaker feels this very paradox even more so as a minister and wishes to leave a spiritual life behind. Yet, when God calls out to him, he is more than willing to respond and continue on.

The paradox is further explored in the very nature of the title itself. The collar means both the collar of a priest and a contraption that

15 rope of sands: Christian limitations on conduct (rope weak like sand) that is changed into "good cable"

16 deaths-head: *n.* a skull; symbolizing mortality

restrains an unruly animal (a sinner perhaps?). The third symbol invoked is the play on words with the homophone “caller”. The caller, of course, being God at the end of the poem.

ROMANCE

George Orwell 1903-1950

When I was young and had no sense
In far-off Mandalay[1]
I lost my heart to a Burmese girl
As lovely as the day.

Her skin was gold, her hair was jet,[2]
Her teeth were ivory;[3]
I said, "for twenty silver pieces,
Maiden, sleep with me".

She looked at me, so pure, so sad,
The loveliest thing alive,
And in her lisping, virgin voice,
Stood out for twenty-five.

1 Mandalay: former capital of Burma (Myanmar)
2 jet: *adj.* black
3 ivory: *adj.* white

HOLY SONNET 14

John Donne 1572-1631

Batter my heart, three-personed God;[1] for You
As yet but knock; breathe, shine, and seek to mend;
That I may rise, and stand, o'erthrow me, and bend
Your force, to break, blow, burn, and make me new.
I, like an usurped[2] town, to another due,
Labor to admit you, but O, to no end.
Reason, your viceroy[3] in me, me should defend,
But is captived, and proves weak or untrue.
Yet dearly I love you, and would be loved fain,[4]
But am betrothed[5] unto your enemy.[6]
Divorce me, untie, or break that knot again,
Take me to you, imprison me, for I,
    Except you enthrall[7] me, never shall be free,
    Nor ever chaste, except you ravish[8] me.

1 three-personed God: The Trinity: God the Father, Jesus the Son, and the Holy Spirit
2 usurped: *adj.* something taken control of by force
3 viceroy: *n.* a person appointed to rule
4 fain: *adv.* willingly
5 betrothed: *adj.* engaged to be married
6 your enemy: The Devil; Satan
7 enthrall: *v.* to enslave
8 ravish: *v.* to violate or rape

TO THE VIRGINS

Robert Herrick 1591-1674

Gather ye rosebuds while ye may,
    Old time is still a-flying;
And the same flower that smiles today
    Tomorrow will be dying.
The glorious lamp of heaven the sun,
    The higher he's a-getting,
The sooner will his race be run,
    And nearer he's to setting.
That age is best which is the first,
    When youth and blood are warmer;
But being spent, the worse, and worst
    Times still succeed the former.
Then be not coy, but use your time,
    And, while ye may, go marry;
For, having lost but once your prime,
    You may forever tarry.

THE WAYFARER

Stephen Crane 1871-1900

The wayfarer,
Perceiving the pathway to truth,
Was struck with astonishment.
It was thickly grown with weeds.
"Ha," he said,
"I see that none has passed here
In a long time."
Later he saw that each weed
Was a singular knife.
"Well," he mumbled at last,
"Doubtless there are other roads."

THE MARRIAGE OF HEAVEN AND HELL

William Blake 1757-1827

Rintrah[1] roars & shakes his fires in the burdened air;
Hungry clouds swag on the deep
Once meek, and in a perilous path,
The just man kept his course along
The vale of death.
Roses are planted where thorns grow,
And on the barren heath[2]
Sing the honey bees.
Then the perilous path was planted,
And a river and a spring
On every cliff and tomb;
And on the bleached bones
Red clay brought forth.
Till the villain left the paths of ease,
To walk in perilous paths, and drive
The just man into barren climes[3].
Now the sneaking serpent walks
In mild humility,
And the just man rages in the wilds
Where lions roam.
Rintrah roars & shakes his fires in the burdened air;
Hungry clouds swag on the deep.

1 Rintrah: the personification of revolutionary wrath in Blake's poetry
2 heath: *n.* a wasteland of bushes and shrubs
3 clime: *n.* climate

RAINBOW

William Wordsworth 1770-1850

My heart leaps up when I behold
A rainbow in the sky:
So was it when my life began;
So is it now I am a man;
So be it when I shall grow old,
Or let me die!
The Child is father of the Man;
I could wish my days to be
Bound each to each by natural piety.

ELEMENT *SIX*:

SYMBOLISM AND ALLEGORY

Introduction to Element Six: Symbolism and Allegory

As has been mentioned previously, denotation is the literal meaning of a word, and connotation is the culmination of various meanings wrapped up in the word. **Symbols** are similar to connotations. Where all words have various connotations that can vary from person to person, their symbols are universally acknowledged. Red usually connotes passion, heat, and anger. However, color an octagon red and place it at an intersection in the road, and we know that it means "stop." That is the power of a symbol. Put a dove on a flag, and we know it means peace. What is somewhat troublesome is the fact that some symbols can have both positive and negative meanings. Let's take the color red again. It can symbolize sin or guilt. Just look at the symbolism of the scarlet letter, an "A" set in red, and the stigma it gave Hester Prynne in Nathanial Hawthorne's **Scarlet Letter**. Caught in adultery, Hester had to wear the red badge as a symbol of her sin and dishonor. Now take the same color and place it on a national flag, and suddenly the symbols changes from dishonor and guilt to sacrifice and courage. So, how do we know what the speaker means? How do we know if the speaker is being literal or symbolic? And if the speaker is being symbolic, which interpretation is the best? The fact that there are no easy answers to these questions shows that richness that poetry offers. The more we read, the easier it is to read symbolism and interpret it more accurately.

Let's now apply symbolism to poetry, particularly to the first few lines from "Do Not Go Gentle into That Good Night" by Dylan Thomas. "Do not go gentle into that good night, / Old age should burn and rage at close of day; / Rage, rage against the dying of the light." When looking at symbols, it is easiest to pick the ones that are simple. First, let's examine "night". Common symbols for night are death, darkness of the soul, and even loss of faith, yet the speaker refers to it as "that good night." Thus, we must reevaluate our symbols. The speaker could mean night as sleep, rest, or death. The next line mentions "old age" and "close of day," so we can start to understand the symbolism more clearly; he is, of course, now referring to death. Then the final line of the stanza reaffirms this symbol: "Rage, rage against the dying of the light." The speaker is speaking to his father who is dying. Death, like the night, can be a cool comfort after the heat and toil of day/life. To many, death is an embrace worth reaching for. The speaker is coaching his dying father, who is fading away into death, to fight twilight that has overcome him, to avoid slipping into the dark depths of death and return to the light of life.

Of course these symbols seem very much like metaphors. How can we distinguish between symbol and metaphor? Let's look at the metaphor "My love is a red rose" again. With this metaphor there is no physical rose present. The speaker is conjuring up an image of a rose for us to compare. Now look at the line from Thomas' poem: "Do not go gentle into that good night." Here, night, as a symbol for death, is physically present, for his father is actually dying and the speaker is comparing night (the symbol) to death (the physical manifestation).

In another symbolic poem "The Sick Rose" by William Blake, the speaker is addressing what appears to be a rose. We know he is speaking symbolically because the rose is present or perhaps the corrupted person that represents the rose:

> O Rose thou art sick!
> The invisible worm
> That flies in the night,
> In the howling storm,
> Has found out thy bed
> Of crimson joy:
> And his dark secret love
> Does thy life destroy.

First, let's look at the symbol of the rose. A rose is an actual living entity, so it can easily symbolize life. The opposite of life is death; thus, the worm that destroys the flower can easily symbolize death. The rest of the poem, however, reveals that these symbols are so much more. We can read the symbol of the rose, which in Blake's poem is symbolic of innocent love, dying at the very hands of rascally nature. "The invisible worm that flies in the night" is not so much the harbinger of death, but love's destructive power. We have seen night being symbolic of death, but here such a symbol does not fit, and it is just refers to the night itself. Just as the serpent was the destructive power in the Garden of Eden by tempting Eve, the destructive worm is somewhat symbolic of the serpent that has secretly come by way of a howling storm to destroy the rose's virginity or innocence. And like some transformations from innocence into experience, the rose knows not of its destruction by the worm. There are sexual connotations in the poem that won't be explored to deeply here, but we can note the rose's "crimson joy," which is sexual in meaning and shows modern culture's attitude toward sex as seen from the Victorian age up to the present. Sex is a natural and beautiful thing that creates life and allows us to continue as a species. Nevertheless, society at large has tainted and shamed the very idea and word of "sex" that it is rarely seen as love but a "dark secret love" that would make grown men and women blush. Thus, "The Sick Rose" is often seen as a symbol of rape, or the dark, destructive power of sex.

As we has seen that metaphors can be extended, so too can symbols. When symbols come together as players on a stage to create an underlying story, they are called **allegory**. Allegory requires understanding all the symbols and how they come together to create a whole new meaning of a moral nature. Abstract concepts are actually personified to create a deeper moral, political, or religious meaning where the abstract ideas that the symbols represent become more important than the symbols themselves. "The Sick Rose" is actually an allegory, where the individual symbols of the rose, the worm, night, and the storm on the surface create the story that is the focus of the poem; however, the underlying symbols of each of these "players" in the poem, create another whole story altogether as has been outlined in the previous paragraph.

Let's examine "Ozymandias" by Percy Bysshe Shelley, which deals with the actual Egyptian pharaoh Ramesses II, or Ozymandias as the Greeks called him.

> I met a traveler from an antique land
> Who said: "Two vast and trunkless[1] legs of stone
> Stand in the desert... Near them, on the sand,
> Half sunk, a shattered visage lies, whose frown,
> And wrinkled lip, and sneer of cold command,
> Tell that its sculptor well those passions read
> Which yet survive, stamped on these lifeless things,
> The hand that mocked them and the heart that fed:
> And on the pedestal these words appear:
> 'My name is Ozymandias,[2] king of kings:
> Look on my works, ye Mighty, and despair!'
> Nothing beside remains. Round the decay
> Of that colossal wreck, boundless and bare
> The lone and level sands stretch far away"

The symbols that Shelley plays with are of power and sovereignty that are usually represented through both the deeds of the mighty and the monuments they leave behind. In the poem a traveler happens upon the ruins of Ozymandias' colossal statue that is nothing more than a pile of stones with the inscription at its ruined feet, "My name is Ozymandias, king of kings: / Look on my works, ye Mighty, and despair!" However, the irony is that the statue is no longer mighty or frightening enough to cause despair. The only thing to despair is the fallen condition of this monument, which has nothing to do with the skill of a mighty pharaoh, but the craft of a lowly sculptor. Art exceeds ambition, as this poem also testifies. In fact, another layer of allegory is that the statue or the symbolism that this fallen statue conjures must despair in the face of the mighty age of modernity.

1 trunkless: *adj.* without a body

2 Ozymandias: the Greek name for the Egyptian pharaoh Ramesses II (1279 BC-1213 BC)

For Shelley, the idea of arrogance common with tyrannical leaders was almost laughable. The poem was written three years after Napoleon Bonaparte's crushing defeat at Waterloo and the demise of the French Empire; what started out as a revolution from tyranny (the French Revolution) that many in England supported, turned into tyranny and oppression again when Napoleon declared himself Emperor. Many, including Shelley, became disheartened by the hope that such a revolution could ever happen in England. In "Ozymandias," Shelley shows that the mighty pharaoh's own efforts to remain immortal throughout history are futile, and Napoleon's efforts, like Ozymandias', will soon end as "a shattered visage." However, the irony of this allegory is not lost, for the name of Ozymandias still lives on as does the memory of his lost civilization, and though this poem is somewhat critical of the pharaoh's arrogance, Ramses continues to live on through the very lines of this poem.

THE TYGER

William Blake 1757-1827

Tyger! Tyger! burning bright
In the forests of the night,
What immortal hand or eye
Could frame thy fearful symmetry?[1]

In what distant deeps or skies
Burnt the fire of thine eyes?
On what wings dare he aspire?[2]
What the hand dare seize the fire?

And what shoulder, & what art.
Could twist the sinews[3] of thy heart?
And when thy heart began to beat,
What dread hand? & what dread feet?

What the hammer? what the chain?
In what furnace was thy brain?
What the anvil? what dread grasp
Dare its deadly terrors clasp?

When the stars threw down their spears,[4]
And watered heaven with their tears,
Did he smile his work to see?
Did he who made the Lamb make thee?

1 symmetry: *n.* shape

2 aspire: *v.* rise up

3 sinew: *n.* muscle; probably meant as strength here

4 the third host of heaven that was cast out with Lucifer in the War in Heaven; Revelations 12:7-10 refers to them as stars

Tyger! Tyger! burning bright
In the forests of the night,
What immortal hand or eye
Dare frame thy fearful symmetry?

KUBLA KAHN[1]

Samuel Taylor Coleridge 1772-1834

In Xanadu[2] did Kubla Khan
A stately pleasure-dome decree:
Where Alph,[3] the sacred river, ran
Through caverns measureless to man
    Down to a sunless sea.
So twice five miles of fertile ground
With walls and towers were girdled[4] round:
And there were gardens bright with sinuous rills,[5]
Where blossomed many an incense-bearing tree;
And here were forests ancient as the hills,
Enfolding sunny spots of greenery.

But oh! that deep romantic chasm which slanted
Down the green hill athwart[6] a cedarn[7] cover!
A savage place! as holy and enchanted
As e'er[8] beneath a waning moon[9] was haunted
By woman wailing for her demon-lover !
And from this chasm, with ceaseless turmoil seething,
As if this earth in fast thick pants were breathing,

---

1 Kubla Kahn: (Kublai Kahn) Mongol Emperor of China (1215-1294); the grandson of Genghis Khan

2 Xanadu: the summer capital in China during Kublai Kahn's dynasty; located in present day inner Mongolia

3 Alph: A mythological underground river that symbolizes sacred knowledge

4 girdle: *v.* to encircle

5 sinuous rills: small, curving rivers

6 athwart: *adv.* crosswise

7 cedarn: *adj.* looking like it was made of cedar or wood

8 e'er: *adv.* poetic form of "ever"

9 waning moon: the moon anytime after it is full

A mighty fountain momently was forced:
Amid whose swift half-intermitted burst
Huge fragments vaulted like rebounding hail,
Or chaffy grain beneath the thresher's[10] flail:
And 'mid these dancing rocks at once and ever
It flung up momently the sacred river.
Five miles meandering with a mazy[11] motion
Through wood and dale the sacred river ran,
Then reached the caverns measureless to man,
And sank in tumult to a lifeless ocean:
And 'mid this tumult Kubla heard from far
Ancestral voices prophesying war!

The shadow of the dome of pleasure
Floated midway on the waves;
Where was heard the mingled measure
From the fountain and the caves.
It was a miracle of rare device,
A sunny pleasure-dome with caves of ice!

A damsel with a dulcimer[12]
In a vision once I saw:
It was an Abyssinian[13] maid,
And on her dulcimer she played,
Singing of Mount Abora.[14]
Could I revive within me
Her symphony and song,

10 thresher: *n.* a person who separates the grain from the plant by beating it during harvest
11 mazy: *adj.* confusing turns like in a maze
12 dulcimer: *n.* a stringed musical instrument
13 Abyssian: Ethiopian (former name)
14 Mount Abora: a mountain range rumored to skirt mythical Xanadu

To such a deep delight 'twould[15] win me,
That with music loud and long,
I would build that dome in air,
That sunny dome! those caves of ice!
And all who heard should see them there,
And all should cry, Beware! Beware!
His flashing eyes, his floating hair!
Weave a circle round him thrice,
And close your eyes with holy dread,
For he on honey-dew hath fed,
And drunk the milk of Paradise.

15 'twould: contraction of "would"

SAILING TO BYZANTIUM[1]

William Butler Yeats 1865-1935

I

That is no country for old men. The young
In one another's arms, birds in the trees
—Those dying generations—at their song,
The salmon-falls,[2] the mackerel-crowded seas,
Fish, flesh, or fowl, commend all summer long
Whatever is begotten, born, and dies.
Caught in that sensual music all neglect
Monuments of unageing intellect.

II

An aged man is but a paltry[3] thing,
A tattered coat upon a stick, unless
Soul clap its hands and sing, and louder sing
For every tatter in its mortal dress,
Nor is there singing school but studying
Monuments of its own magnificence;
And therefore I have sailed the seas and come
To the holy city of Byzantium.

III

O sages standing in God's holy fire
As in the gold mosaic[4] of a wall,

1 Byzantium: an ancient Greek city that was rebuilt by Constantine in 330 and renamed Constantinople (modern day Istanbul, Turkey), the New Rome, and the capital of the Holy Roman Empire that became the largest and wealthiest city in the Middle Ages

2 salmon-falls: referencing how salmon swim up river, even up small waterfalls, to spawn

3 paltry: *adj.* worthless

Come from the holy fire, perne in a gyre[5],
And be the singing-masters of my soul.
Consume my heart away; sick with desire
And fastened to a dying animal
It knows not what it is; and gather me
Into the artifice of eternity.

IV
Once out of nature I shall never take
My bodily form from any natural thing,
But such a form as Grecian[6] goldsmiths make
Of hammered gold and gold enameling
To keep a drowsy Emperor awake;
Or set upon a golden bough to sing
To lords and ladies of Byzantium
Of what is past, or passing, or to come.

4 mosaic: *n.* pieces of colored glass that creates an image; many found in the cathedrals of Constantinople

5 perne in a gyre: many critics debate the meaning of this word; perhaps spinning wheel image where the wheel spins both sides of a paper faster than the human eye can detect to create an image

6 Grecian: Greek

VIRTUE

George Herbert 1593-1633

Sweet day, so cool, so calm, so bright,
The bridal of the earth and sky;
The dew shall weep thy fall tonight,
For thou must die.

Sweet rose, whose hue angry and brave[1]
Bids the rash gazer wipe his eye;
Thy root is ever in its grave,
And thou must die.

Sweet spring, full of sweet days and roses,
A box where sweets compacted lie;
My music shows ye have your closes,[2]
And all must die.

Only a sweet and virtuous soul,
Like seasoned timber, never gives;
But though the whole world turn to coal,[3]
Then chiefly lives.

1 angry and brave: metaphors for red and magnificent

2 closes: referring to the final cadence of the music

3 whole world turn to coal: referring to the world burning to cinders at the Final Judgment of God

UPHILL

Christina Rossetti 1830-1894

Does the road wind up-hill all the way?
    Yes, to the very end.
Will the day's journey take the whole long day?
    From morn[1] to night, my friend.
But is there for the night a resting-place?
    A roof for when the slow dark hours begin.
May not the darkness hide it from my face?
    You cannot miss that inn.

Shall I meet other wayfarers at night?
    Those who have gone before.
Then must I knock, or call when just in sight?
    They will not keep you standing at that door.

Shall I find comfort, travel-sore and weak?
    Of labor you shall find the sum.
Will there be beds for me and all who seek?
    Yea, beds for all who come.

---

1 morn: *n.* morning

FIRE AND ICE

Robert Frost 1874-1963

Some say the world will end in fire,
Some say in ice.
From what I've tasted of desire
I hold with those who favor fire.
But if it had to perish twice,
I think I know enough of hate
To say that for destruction ice
Is also great
And would suffice.

ELEMENT *SEVEN*: SYNTAX

Introduction to Element Seven: Syntax

Syntax is best explained as how the words are arranged in any given sentence. Poetry is well suited for the rearrangement of syntax. While the vocabulary can be common and easy to understand, the syntax found in poetry can lead to misunderstanding and confusion, especially for students learning English as another language. For example, William Butler Yeats starts his poem "The Lake Isle of Innisfree" with uncommon syntax. "I will arise and go now, and go to Innisfree, / And a small cabin build there, of clay and wattles made." We would not encounter such a structure in prose unless the writer was also trying to be poetic. A more common way to write the sentence is "I will arise and go now to Innisfree and build a small cabin of clay and wattles." Obviously, the sentence I just wrote is not as creative as Yeats'. The reason why Yeats changes the syntax to an unorthodox structure is to manipulate the tone, and give us a glimpse into the speaker's state of mind. The repetition of "go" reveals how the speaker is feeling; there is a sense of urgency for leaving, dissatisfaction over the current status quo. This is similar to how we may speak to a friend on the phone. The conversation is going on too long, and we feel urgency in stopping the call and moving on. We may speak as thus: "I've gotta go now, gotta go to the store before it closes." The repetition not only reveals our state of urgency, but also our need to excuse ourselves from the present predicament.

In the second line, Yeats changes the syntax completely to describe the cabin. One of the obvious reasons is to shift focus onto the cabin, which is the heart of the stanza. It is interesting to note that the object of the sentence comes before the verbs. Poets use this form of **passive voice** to downplay who is responsible for something. Here the speaker wishes to emphasize the cabin and what it is built of, not who built it. He also rearranges the syntax to meet the meter of 13 syllables per line that he has established for the first three lines of each stanza.

Another common type of poetic syntax is the **ellipsis**, or leaving words out of sentences where the reader usually expects to read them. For example, in "Preludes" by T.S. Eliot, the poet utilizes ellipsis to keep meter in his poem: "You curled the papers from **your** hair, / Or clasped the yellow soles of feet / In the palms of both soiled hands." I emphasized "your" in the first line. Can you see where ellipsis is used in the following lines? "Your" is omitted in the following two lines. Correct grammar would be written as "*your* feet" and "*your* soiled hands." Try to find ellipsis in Thomas Hardy's "The Darkling Thrush."

> The land's sharp features seemed to be
> The Century's corpse outleant,[1]
> His crypt the cloudy canopy,
> The wind his death-lament.

Look for features in the first line that can be repeated in the last two lines. Can you see it? Take the form "seemed to be" that is used to link the first line to the second. Ellipsis is used to omit the grammatical feature to create conciseness without losing meaning. The third and fourth line should read, "His crypt *seemed to be* the cloudy canopy, / The wind *seemed to be* his death-lament."

Let's look at Robert Frost's poem "The Silken Tent" as another example of syntax used for poetic means.

> She is as in a field a silken tent
> At midday when the sunny summer breeze
> Has dried the dew and all its ropes relent,[2]
> So that in guys[3] it gently sways at ease,

1 outleant: poetic form meaning 'lean out'
2 relent: *v.* slacken
3 guy: *n.* a rope used secure a tent

And its supporting central cedar pole,
That is its pinnacle to heavenward
And signifies the sureness of the soul,
Seems to owe naught[4] to any single cord,
But strictly held by none, is loosely bound
By countless silken ties of love and thought
To everything on earth the compass round,[5]
And only by one's going slightly taut
In the capriciousness[6] of summer air
Is of the slightest bondage made aware.

What is the first thing you notice about the syntax of the poem? The entire poem is one compound-complex sentence. Look at the poem again and notice there are only commas at the end the lines and the period is not used until the last line. How does Frost make the poem comprehensible as one sentence? He uses the conjunctions **so** (line 4), *and* (line 5), *And* (line 7), *But* (line 9), as well as *And* (line 12). Using these conjunctions allows the reader to move from one clause to the next without losing context or understanding. The first three lines make a complex sentence connected by the subordinator *when* and is fairly straightforward to understand. The complexity comes in lines 4-14. Line 4 continues the previous complex sentence with the subordinator *So that* with "it gently sways at ease" as the clause to follow. Line 5 uses *And* to create another independent clause with "its supporting central cedar pole" being the subject of the clause with the main verb "seems" not appearing until line 8, while line 6 and 7 serve only as an adjective clause. Frost reverses the syntax of line 13 and 14 to maintain final rhyming couplet. It should correctly read, "In the capriciousness of summer air is made aware of the slightest bondage."

Finally, syntax in poetry is the poet's ability to break the sentences into discrete parts. Traditional poetry was more conventional, but the way poets punctuate and break the lines of their poems is not really

4 naught: *n.* nothing
5 the compass round: in every direction on the compass; north, east, south, and west
6 capriciousness: *n.* erratic; directionless

understood. How a poet writes a poem is just as important as the meaning. Let's look at Lord Tennyson's "The Eagle" again to see the various ways it can be written. The first two lines are fairly straight-forward.

> He clasps the crag with crooked hands;
> Close to the sun in lonely lands,

These lines paint a very clear picture of an eagle standing on a cliff, high in the sky. Notice the ellipsis in the second line. It should read, "He stands close to the sun in lonely lands." The poet could change the punctuation around to affect the overall meaning of the poem:

> he clasps the crag... with crooked hands?
> close to the sun in lonely lands.

Though the words in the poem haven't changed, the meaning has by adding a bit of humor and maybe even irony through use of the three dots, also known as **ellipsis**, and the inclusion of a question mark at the end of the first line to replace the semicolon. With the capitals removed, the style of the poem is also altered into a more non-traditional form as is more common with the poet E.E. Cummings (also written ee cummings). The question mark also actively involves the reader to interpret the eagle's actions by agreeing or disagreeing with the speaker's suggestion that the eagle may or may not have crooked hands. It draws attention to the personification of the bird and questions the speakers overall usage of such a metaphor in a light, or humorous way. The poems syntax can be altered in a different way as well.

> He clasps the crags
> With "crooked hands;"
> Close to the sun
> In lonely lands!

The two lines have now been turned into four. The placing of quotations around "crooked hands" adds a moniker to the eagle as if this is unique to only this bird the speaker is discussing. The insertion of the exclamation mark at the end of the poem adds a surprise that both the speaker and reader share, the fact that there is nothing in the air or land for the regal bird to hunt.

As you can see, the syntactic style of a poem can change the overall meaning as well. We, as conscientious readers, need to pay closer attention to the syntax structures on the page to help our overall interpretation of the poem. This is what makes poetry so much more fluid and exciting than prose.

THE GREAT FIGURE

William Carlos Williams 1883-1963

Among the rain
and lights
I saw the figure 5
in gold
on a red
firetruck
moving
tense
unheeded
to gong clangs
siren howls
and wheels rumbling
through the dark city

I HEARD A FLY BUZZ

Emily Dickenson 1830-1886

I heard a Fly buzz—when I died—
The Stillness in the Room
Was like the stillness in the Air—
Between the Heaves[1] of Storm—

The Eyes[2] around—had wrung them dry—
And breaths were gathering firm
For that last Onset—when the King
Be witnessed—in the Room—

I willed my Keepsakes—Signed away
What portion of me be
Assignable[3]—and then it was
There interposed a fly—

With Blue—uncertain stumbling Buzz—
Between the light—and me—
And then the Windows failed—and then
I could not see to see[4]—

1 heaves: *n.* tumultuousness

2 the Eyes: the loved ones standing over the speaker's body

3 here the speaker is referencing he will and all that she will give away upon her death

4 I could not see to see: the speaker finally dies

WHEN I WAS ONE-AND-TWENTY

A.E. Housman 1859-1936

When I was one-and-twenty
    I heard a wise man say,
"Give crowns and pounds and guineas[1]
    But not your heart away;
Give pearls away and rubies
    But keep your fancy free."
But I was one-and-twenty,
    No use to talk to me.

When I was one-and-twenty
    I heard him say again,
  "The heart out of the bosom[2]
    Was never given in vain;

'Tis paid with sighs a plenty
    And sold for endless rue.[3]"
And I am two-and-twenty,
    And oh, 'tis true, 'tis true.

---

1 guinea: *n.* a gold coin used in the United Kingdom before 1830
2 bosom: *n.* chest
3 rue: *n.* sorrow or regret

POETRY[1]

Marianne Moore 1887-1972

I, too, dislike it: there are things that are important
beyond all this fiddle.[2]
Reading it, however, with a perfect contempt for it,
one discovers that there is in
it after all, a place for the genuine.
Hands that can grasp, eyes
that can dilate,[3] hair that can rise
if it must, these things are important not be-
cause a

high sounding interpretation can be put upon them
but because they are
useful; when they become so derivative[4] as to
become unintelligible, the
same thing may be said for all of us – that we
do not admire what
we cannot understand. The bat,
holding on upside down or in quest of some-
thing to

eat, elephants pushing, a wild horse taking a roll,
a tireless wolf under
a tree, the immovable critic twinkling his skin like a

1 1921 version
2 fiddle: informal British meaning ‘fraud’
3 dilate: *v.* to become larger
4 derivative: *adj.* secondary; unoriginal

horse that feels a flea, the base-
ball fan, the statistician — case after case
could be cited did
one wish it; nor is it valid
to discriminate against "business documents
and

school-books"; all these phenomena are important.
One must make a distinction
however: when dragged into prominence by half
poets,
the result is not poetry,
nor till the autocrats[5] among us can be
"literalists of
the imagination" – above
insolence and triviality and can present

for inspection, imaginary gardens with real toads
in them, shall we have
it. In the meantime, if you demand on one hand,
in defiance of their opinion –
the raw material of poetry in
all its rawness, and
that which is on the other hand,
genuine, then you are interested in poetry.

5 autocrat: *n.* a person claiming absolute authority; Moore is speaking of poets

IN JUST-

e.e. cummings 1894-1962

in Just-
spring   when the world is mud-
luscious[1] the little
lame balloonman

whistles   far   and wee[2]

and eddieandbill[3] come
running from marbles and
piracies[4] and it's
spring

when the world is puddle-wonderful

the queer
old balloonman whistles
far   and   wee
and bettyandisbel[5] come dancing

from hop-scotch and jump-rope and

it's
spring

1 mud-luscious: luscious means 'satisfying to the senses'; thus the mud created after the rain becomes a child's playground
2 wee: *adj.* very small; miniscule; a play on the term 'far and wide'
3 eddieandbill: Eddie and Bill; the children in the poem
4 piracies: symbolic for all the trouble children get into
5 bettyandisbel: Betty and Isbel; more children

and
the

goat-footed

balloonMan   whistles[6]
far
and
wee

6 goat-footed balloonMan whistles: a reference to Pan, god of nature in Greek myth; he had goats feet and played (whistled) a pipe; by adding balloonMan, Cummings modernizes the classical Greek satyr

I SHOT GATSBY[1]

Steven Lynn Reeder 1972~

Sitting alone on an ash heap,
My wife has cockled me again
I don't know who it is that she[2] is with;
All I know is that she has distanced herself from me...
I shot Gatsby.

My friend Tom[3] came in a "yellow circus wagon,"
Not the blue coupe that he promised me.
Eckleburg's eyes[4] bore down on me;
I shivered as Tom swaggered around the car...
Liar.

But it was his look that stabbed my heart;
I turned away; Myrtle's eyes became Eckleburg's.
I hit my wife though it broke my heart;
I had to show her that I really lover her...
Really!

She shed a tear and fled to her room;
I sat in shadow and brewed my swollen heart.
Now I hear the motor; I see my wife,
A specter in the gloom run out into the night
I knew it!

1 Gastsby: the protagonist of F. Scott Fizgerald's *The Great Gatsby* (1925)

2 she: referencing Myrtle, the speaker's, the George Wilson's wife

3 Tom: Tom Buchanan, the husband of Daisy, Gatsby's love interest; Tom is also having an affair with Myrtle

4 Eckleburg's eyes: a painted advertisement of giant eyes and glasses of Dr. Eckleburg, an optician

She screams to escape; she wails out in pain.
The yellow wagon[5] bounces over her delicate form.
The police come and ask obnoxious questions.
Tom follows in their wake, and swear he never was[6]...
Liar!

I grab my gun, and stalk to his place.
The taste of metal makes him confess[7] to me.
Outside the mansion[8], I stamp on his flowers;
I draw my pistol and enter his solitude.
I'm shooting Gatsby!

He is sitting in his pool so smug.
I am so revolted, I pull the trigger hard.
The blood flows in a bloom out of his head;
My soul tries to scream; I put a bullet there instead[9]
...

5 yellow wagon: this is Gatsby's roadster again, and this time Daisy is driving it after Gatsby professes his love to her; she accidentally runs over Myrtle thinking it is Tom driving to take her away

6 The speaker thinks Tom was the driver of the roadster; but he, of course, flatly denies it.

7 The speaker threatens Tom with a gun and he confesses that Gatsby was driving the roadster. Earlier in the novel, Gatsby lies to Tom about driving the car to protect Daisy.

8 Tom goes to Gatsby's mansion to kill him

9 After shooting Gatsby, the speaker then kills himself with the same gun.

ELEMENT *EIGHT*:
IMAGERY

Introduction to Element Eight: Imagery

A popular mantra of all writers is "show; don't tell." This is particularly the case for poets. Their duty is to show us worlds of sight, sound, taste, smell, and touch in exact detail. Thus, we, as readers, need to read not only with our eyes, but with our ears as well. The words in poems create images and feelings that need to be understood on various levels. An **image** accurately depicts our senses, emotions, or thoughts in a way that all can understand. We spend most of our days looking at the world through a dirty window pane. Poets are like window washers clearing away our obscure view of the world and even opening the window so that we can sense the world around us with greater clarity. This is the way of poetry, to make the world seem clearer. By doing so, poems may generate memories long forgotten, excite feelings we thought never existed, and sway responses in directions we rarely go.

Poets elicit images to create such details in the mind's eye. How would you explain rush hour in a subway station with such clarity that only one sentence is needed? Ezra Pound tried it with his very short poem "In a Station in the Metro."

> The apparition[1] of these faces in the crowd;
> Petals on a wet, black bough.

Here Pound attempts to capture an experience he had in a Paris subway where, upon exiting the train, he noticed faces that were beautiful to behold. He suffered for a year over the image, trying to put into

1 apparition: *n.* appearance

words what he experienced. He went from a thirty line poem to a fifteen line poem and destroyed both, knowing that they did not capture the portrait-like event that he had observed with such clarity. What he decided upon is best put into his own words, "In a poem of this sort one is trying to record the precise instant when a thing outward and objective transforms itself, or darts into a thing inward and subjective.[2]" When he finished he managed to produce a photogenic piece of poetry that *showed* us the sensory experience of that day and not just *telling* us. By describing the faces of the crowd as an apparition, there is something ghostly and out of focus of what the speaker is seeing, and those faces are likened to petals on a wet, black branch. What the speaker has seen is something bright, wondrous, and alive, in dark, wet subway stations; something beautiful has grown out of despair.

Let's look at something other than just the visual image. T.S. Eliot was the master of bringing images out of the Romantic era of beauty and nature to record what we experience in the everyday dirt and grime of our city streets. Notice the attention to detail the poet gives to not only the visual images, but others as well in "The Winter Evening Settles Down."

> The winter evening settles down
> With smells of steaks in passageways.
> Six o'clock.
> The burnt-out ends of smoky days.
> And now a gusty shower wraps
> The grimy scraps
> Of withered leaves across your feet
> And newspapers from vacant lots;
> The showers beat
> On empty blinds and chimney-pots,
> And at the corner of the street
> A lonely cab-horse steams and stamps.
>
> And then the lighting of the lamps.

2 See http://rpo.library.utoronto.ca/poem/1657.html

Notice how the images of winter are altered when taken from the refreshing images of peace and tranquility surrounded by a blanket of crystal white snow to the cold, dirty reality of city streets. Winter in London is far from enjoyable; it is often cold and bitter. Add a winter rain, and it becomes absolutely miserable. Eliot wonderfully describes concrete images of burnt-out cigarettes, grimy garbage, withered leaves, and empty blinds and chimney pots to conjure a world of sterility and destruction. He conjures all sorts of sensory perceptions: the smell of steaks cooking; the feel of grimy scraps of withered leaves; the sound of rain beating on windows and chimneys; the sight of someone lighting the city lamps. These are called **concrete** images, for they stimulate senses directly as if we were actually there to witness the scene.

A second type of image is called **abstract**. Words like sadness, fear, excitement, and courage have meanings that cannot be experienced through the five senses and have different meanings for individual readers. For example, in William Wordsworth's poem "It is a Beauteous Evening" he writes:

> It is a beauteous evening, calm and free,
> The holy time is quiet as a Nun
> Breathless with adoration; the broad sun
> Is sinking down in its tranquility;

Compare the language here with that of Eliot's and we can see a clear distinction between concrete (Eliot's) and abstract (Wordsworth's) images. If I were to ask a group of people to conjure the smell of steaks cooking in passageways, all would have the same sensory idea. This is concrete. Now, if I were to ask the same group to conjure the vision of a beauteous evening, all would have different sensory perceptions of what that would be like. This is what is meant by **abstract**. How can we pinpoint "holy time" or "adoration" or even "tranquility"? To each and every one of us, these words have only personal abstract meanings. Poems that use abstract imagery create excellent connotations as discussed in Element Four: Diction.

ODE ON A GRECIAN URN

John Keats 1795-1821

1

Thou still unravished[1] bride of quietness,
Thou foster-child of silence and slow time,
Sylvan[2] historian, who canst thus express
A flowery tale more sweetly than our rhyme:
What leaf-fringed legend haunt about thy shape
Of deities or mortals, or of both,
In Tempe[3] or the dales of Arcady?[4]
What men or gods are these? What maidens loth?[5]
What mad pursuit? What struggle to escape?
What pipes and timbrels?[6] What wild ecstasy?

2

Heard melodies are sweet, but those unheard
Are sweeter: therefore, ye soft pipes, play on;
Not to the sensual ear, but, more endeared,
Pipe to the spirit ditties[7] of no tone:
Fair youth, beneath the trees, thou canst not leave
Thy song, nor ever can those trees be bare;
Bold lover, never, never canst thou kiss,
Though winning near the goal - yet, do not grieve;
She cannot fade, though thou hast not thy bliss,

1 unravished: *adj.* virgin
2 sylvan: *adj.* a person or thing that lives in the woods
3 Tempe: a valley in eastern Greece
4 Arcady: the poetic form of Arcadia, a mountain range in ancient Greece
5 loth: *adj.* unwilling
6 timbrel: *n.* a tambourine
7 ditty: a poem that is sung

For ever wilt thou love, and she be fair!

3

Ah, happy, happy boughs! that cannot shed
Your leaves, nor ever bid the spring adieu;[8]
And, happy melodist, unwearied,
For ever piping songs for ever new;
More happy love! more happy, happy love!
For ever warm and still to be enjoyed,
For ever panting, and for ever young;
All breathing human passion far above,
That leaves a heart high-sorrowful and cloyed,[9]
A burning forehead, and a parching tongue.

4

Who are these coming to the sacrifice?
To what green altar, O mysterious priest,
Lead'st thou that heifer[10] lowing[11] at the skies,
And all her silken flanks with garlands[12] dressed?
What little town by river or sea shore,
Or mountain-built with peaceful citadel,
Is emptied of this folk, this pious morn?[13]
And, little town, thy streets for evermore
Will silent be; and not a soul to tell
Why thou art desolate, can e'er[14] return.

8 adieu: good-bye
9 cloy: *v.* to be weary of pleasure
10 heifer: *n.* a young cow
11 low: *v.* moo; the sound a cow makes
12 garland: *n.* a wreath of flowers
13 morn: poetic form of 'morning'
14 e'er: ever; used to turn a two syllable word into one

5

O Attic[15] shape! Fair attitude! with brede[16]
    Of marble men[17] and maidens overwrought,
With forest branches and the trodden weed;
    Thou, silent form, dost tease us out of thought
As doth eternity: Cold Pastoral![18]
    When old age shall this generation waste,
        Thou shalt remain, in midst of other woe
    Than ours, a friend to man, to whom thou say'st,
"Beauty is truth, truth beauty," — that is all
        Ye know on earth, and all ye need to know.

---

15 Attic: relating to Athens, Greece

16 brede: *n.* old form meaning 'something braided'

17 marble men: men painted on the marble urn

18 Cold Pastoral: a pastoral is a picture of country life; cold pastoral refers to a pastoral picture on a cold lifeless urn

THE LAKE ISLE OF INNISFREE

William Butler Yeats 1865-1939

I will arise and go now, and go to Innisfree,[1]
And a small cabin build there, of clay and wattles[2] made:
Nine bean-rows will I have there, a hive for the honey-bee,
And live alone in the bee-loud glade.

And I shall have some peace there, for peace comes dropping slow,
Dropping from the veils of the morning to where the cricket sings;
There midnight's all a glimmer, and noon a purple glow,
And evening full of the linnet's[3] wings.

I will arise and go now, for always night and day
I hear lake water lapping[4] with low sounds by the shore;
While I stand on the roadway, or on the pavements grey,
I hear it in the deep heart's core.

1 Innisfree: located in Ireland
2 wattle: *n.* sticks interwoven together to make a wall
3 linnet: *n.* a small bird
4 lap: *v.* water washing up against something

CHICAGO[1]

Carl Sandburg 1878-1967

Hog Butcher for the World,
Tool Maker, Stacker of Wheat,
Player with Railroads and the Nation's Freight Handler;
Stormy, husky, brawling,
City of the Big Shoulders:[2]

They tell me you are wicked and I believe them, for I have seen your painted women under the gas lamps[3] luring the farm boys.
And they tell me you are crooked and I answer: Yes, it is true I have seen the gunman[4] kill and go free to kill again.
And they tell me you are brutal and my reply is: On the faces of women and children I have seen the marks of wanton hunger.
And having answered so I turn once more to those who sneer at this my city, and I give them back the sneer and say to them:
Come and show me another city with lifted head singing so proud to be alive and coarse[5] and strong and cunning.
Flinging magnetic curses amid the toil of piling job on

1 Chicago: a city in the state of Illinois; the third largest city in the U.S.
2 all the professions listed is what made Chicago famous in the 1920's, a city of big shoulders means a city of manual laborers
3 painted women under glass lamps: prostitutes
4 gunmen: the notorious Chicago gangsters such as Al Capone
5 coarse: *adj.* vulgar; crude

job, here is a tall bold slugger[6] set vivid against the
little soft cities;

Fierce as a dog with tongue lapping for action, cunning
as a savage pitted against the wilderness,
Bareheaded,
Shoveling,
Wrecking,
Planning,
Building, breaking, rebuilding,
Under the smoke, dust all over his mouth, laughing with
white teeth,
Under the terrible burden of destiny laughing as a young
man laughs,
Laughing even as an ignorant fighter laughs who has
never lost a battle,
Bragging and laughing that under his wrist is the pulse.
and under his ribs the heart of the people,
Laughing!
Laughing the stormy, husky, brawling laughter of
Youth, half-naked, sweating, proud to be Hog
Butcher, Tool Maker, Stacker of Wheat, Player with
Railroads and Freight Handler to the Nation.

6 slugger: *n.* boxer

GOD'S GRANDEUR

Gerard Manley Hopkins 1844-1889

The World is charged with the grandeur of God.
    It will flame out, like shining from shook foil;
    It gathers to a greatness, like the ooze of oil
Crushed. Why do men then now not reck[1] his rod?[2]
Generations have trod, have trod, have trod;
    And all is seared with trade; bleared, smeared with toil;
    And wears man's smudge and shares man's smell: the soil
Is bare now, nor can foot feel, being shod.[3]

And for all this, nature is never spent;
    There lives the dearest freshness deep down things;
And though the last lights off the black West went
    Oh, morning, at the brown brink eastward, springs—
Because the Holy Ghost[4] over the bent
    World broods with warm breast and with ah! bright wings.

1 reck: *v.* old form meaning 'to have regard for' or 'to obey'

2 rod: *n.* a stick of authority; often used in the Bible to connote God's authority

3 shod: *adj.* provided with shoes

4 Holy Ghost: the holy spirit of the Trinity (Godhead): God the father, Jesus, the son, and the holy spirit;

MEETING AT NIGHT

Robert Browning 1812-1889

I.
The grey sea and the long black land;
And the yellow half-moon large and low;
And the startled little waves that leap
In fiery ringlets from their sleep,
As I gain the cove with pushing prow,
And quench its speed i' the slushy sand.

II.
Then a mile of warm sea-scented beach;
Three fields to cross till a farm appears;
A tap at the pane, the quick sharp scratch
And blue spurt of a lighted match,
And a voice less loud, thro' its joys and fears,
Than the two hearts beating each to each!

AMONG SCHOOL CHILDREN

William Butler Yeats 1865-1939

I

I walk through the long schoolroom questioning;
A kind old nun in a white hood replies;
The children learn to cipher and to sing,
To study reading-books and histories,
To cut and sew, be neat in everything
In the best modern way — the children's eyes
In momentary wonder stare upon
A sixty-year-old smiling public man.

II

I dream of a Ledaean[1] body, bent
Above a sinking fire, a tale that she
Told of a harsh reproof, or trivial event
That changed some childish day to tragedy —
Told, and it seemed that our two natures blent[2]
Into a sphere from youthful sympathy,
Or else, to alter Plato's[3] parable,
Into the yolk and white of the one shell.

III

And thinking of that fit of grief or rage
I look upon one child or t'other there

1 Ledaean: a reference to Leda, who was raped by Zeus in the form of the swan. Ledaean means 'of the swan' and is a reference to the beauty and grandeur of Helen, the daughter of Leda, whose beauty sparked the Trojan War

2 blent: *v.* a variant of blended

3 Plato: a Greek philosopher from 5th century B.C.; a pupil of Socrates

And wonder if she stood so at that age—
For even daughters of the swan can share
Something of every paddler's heritage—
And had that color upon cheek or hair,
And thereupon my heart is driven wild:
She stands before me as a living child.

IV
Her present image floats into the mind—
Did Quattrocento[4] finger fashion it
Hollow of cheek as though it drank the wind
And took a mess of shadows for its meat?
And I though never of Ledaean kind
Had pretty plumage once—enough of that,
Better to smile on all that smile, and show
There is a comfortable kind of old scarecrow.[5]

V
What youthful mother, a shape upon her lap
Honey of generation had betrayed,
And that must sleep, shriek, struggle to escape
As recollection or the drug decide,
Would think her Son, did she but see that shape
With sixty or more winters on its head,
A compensation for the pang of his birth,
Or the uncertainty of his setting forth?

VI
Plato thought nature but a spume[6] that plays

4 Quattrocento: an Italian artistic style of the Middle Ages
5 old scarecrow: the speaker refers to himself as such
6 spume: *n.* foam

Upon a ghostly paradigm of things;
Solider Aristotle[7] played the taws[8]
Upon the bottom of a king of kings;[9]
World-famous golden-thighed Pythagoras[10]
Fingered upon a fiddle-stick or strings
What a star sang and careless Muses heard:
Old clothes upon old sticks to scare a bird.[11]

VII

Both nuns and mothers worship images,
But those the candles light are not as those
That animate a mother's reveries,
But keep a marble or a bronze repose.
And yet they too break hearts — O presences
That passion, piety or affection knows,
And that all heavenly glory symbolize —
O self-born mockers of man's enterprise;

VIII

Labor is blossoming or dancing where
The body is not bruised to pleasure soul.
Nor beauty born out of its own despair,
Nor blear-eyed wisdom out of midnight oil.
O chestnut-tree, great-rooted blossomer,
Are you the leaf, the blossom or the bole?[12]

7 Aristotle: Greek philosopher and student to Plato; accompanied Alexander the Great on his military campaigns as his teacher and historian

8 taws: *n.* a leather whip often used to punish school children

9 king of kings: a reference to Alexander the Great who conquered most of the known (Western) world

10 Pythagoras: Greek philosopher and musician 6th century BC who, according to Plato, had a thigh of gold, a sign of divinity, especially an offspring of the god Apollo

11 old clothes upon sticks...bird: (just skin and bones) another reference to a scarecrow, to which the speaker had also referenced himself

O body swayed to music, O brightening glance,
How can we know the dancer from the dance?

---

12 bole: *n.* the trunk of a tree

ELEMENT *NINE*:
RHYTHM AND METER

Introduction to Element *Nine*: Rhythm and Meter

Rhythm in poetry is like beating a drum; stressed and unstressed syllables create a definitive beat. Historically, poetry developed from its natural tendency to mimic everyday life; from the lock/step of walking to the pulse beating of our hearts, even the regulated cadence of breathing adds a sense of perpetual rhythm to our existence. Rhythm is part of our lives, which is why poetry and songs have been so much a part of civilization. Furthermore, the natural rhythm of speech is regulated by meter, and in poetry it controls the regular beat of the lines to the point of predictability.

The natural rises and falls of lines in poetry is regulated by meter; this is called stress and allows the speaker's voice to rise and hesitate but a moment on that stressed syllable. Stress is what creates the natural rhythm in words and brings out the beats associated with poetry and song like in waTER, LIberTY, SEAson, and GETting. When these words are strung together in sentences then an underlying rhythm is established where the stressed syllables (those shown in capitals) become prominent as in the famous Shakespearean quote, "to BE or NOT to BE, THAT is the QUEStion."

As has been hinted on in previous chapters, the usage or breaking of this rhythm helps the poet to convey various meanings or feelings. Let's take the example from the first stanza of William Blake's poem "The Tyger."

> TYger TYger, BURNing BRIGHT
> IN the FORests OF the NIGHT
> WHAT imMORtal HAND or EYE
> could FRAME thy FEARful SYMmeTRY

Blake's poem consists of exact rhymes, but the final two lines of this first stanza, which is also repeated in the last stanza, create this half rhyme (see element 11) that should not be forced to rhyme. Here is a case where the break in exact rhyme creates irony, for the speaker breaks the symmetry of the stanza by not only changing the rhythm but also to use the word symmetry, which also adds an extra syllable! Each line has seven syllables, but this last line has eight.

Now that we understand that words and sentences have a rhythm to them established through their syllables, we can now move on to meter. **Meter** creates the basic structure of the rhythm in a poem. We look at the stressed and unstressed syllables in a set length within a line. A poem with a line of ten syllables (the set length of line) may have the first syllable as unstressed, the second as stressed, the third as unstressed, and so on until the stressed tenth syllable at the end of the line. Shakespeare often wrote this style of line. Let's look at a famous line from *Romeo and Juliet*.

1 2 3 4 5
but SOFT!/ what LIGHT/ through YON/der WIN/dow BREAKS?

The combination of stressed/unstressed syllables makes up a **foot**. The line of ten syllables has five feet. The stressed/unstressed combination is called an **iamb**; five feet is called **pentameter** (penta [5] + meter [rhythmic unit]). Thus, this type of common line is called **iambic pentameter**. Furthermore, the dividing of poetic lines into feet and indicating the stress and unstressed parts is called **scansion** and is an important part of a critical analysis of a poem. Let's look at the most common types of meter in poetry.

STRESSES	FOOT	SYLLABLES	METER
Unstressed + Stressed (rising)	Iamb	Two	Iambic
Stressed + Unstressed (falling)	Trochee	Two	Trochaic
Stressed + Stressed (substitute)	Spondee	Two	Spondaic
Unstressed + Unstressed + Stressed (rising)	Anapest	Three	Anapestic
Stressed + Unstressed + Unstressed (falling)	Dactyl	Three	Dactylic

Next, we need to understand the different types of meter in the line, or how many feet are used.

METRICAL LINE	METRICAL FOOT
Monometer	One
Dimeter	Two
Trimeter	Three
Tetrameter	Four
Penatameter	Five
Hexameter	Six
Heptameter	Seven
Octameter	Eight

When we analyze the rhythmic meter of a poem, we take into account the rhythmic unit and the feet. Let's look at the first line of William Butler Yeats' poem.

1 2 3 4
LAY your / SLEEPing / HEAD, my / LOVE

Because it is stressed/unstressed with two syllables, it is a trochee. It also has four feet, so it is in tetrameter. Thus, we can say that Yeats' poem is written in **trochaic tetrameter**. You may have noticed that the first three feet have two syllables each, while the last foot has only one stressed syllable. This is called **catalexis**, and it is not a full foot. So, the proper term for this poem is actually **trochaic tetrameter catalectic**. William Blake's "The Tyger" is the same as well. Can you see the pattern? If the first three lines of "The Tyger" are the same, then what do we call the last line that has eight syllables instead of seven?

1 2 3 4
could FRAME / thy FEAR/ful SYM/meTRY

It has unstressed/stressed rhythm of two syllables with four feet. Thus, it must be **iambic tetrameter**. Where the first three lines had a catalexis, this final line does not and is a full foot.

Let's look at another example of meter from another poem. Here are two lines from the introduction to Henry Wadsworth Longfellow's **Evangeline.**

> This is the forest primeval. The murmuring pines and the hemlocks,
> Bearded with moss, and in garments green, indistinct in the twilight,

You may have noticed as you read that the falling stress is like a rolling of the waves near the shore—RISE, fall, fall / RISE, fall, fall. The rhythm could rock you to sleep. So why doesn't poetry put the reader to sleep? Poets are well adept at varying the meter in their poems.

> THIS is the / FORest prim / EVal. the / MURmuring / PINES and the / HEMlocks.
> BEARDed with / MOSS, and in / GARments green, / INdistinct / in the TWI / light,

The first line has the stressed unstressed unstressed feet of three syllables making it a dactyl. It is also broken into six metrical feet of a hexameter, scanning in **dactylic hexameter**. Note the catalexis of the final unfinished foot "hemlocks." In the second line the final foot is rising and anapestic. This breaks the monotony of the poem, but still keeps the rhythm intact.

Now we can understand how to read poems more proficiently. Just because a line ends, does not mean we pause. Punctuation indicates places of pause, not the end of lines. Punctuation at the end of lines indicates natural pauses, otherwise known as an **end stopped line**; however, punctuation within the line is called **caesura** and will be indicated with a double slash (//). Let's look at the beginning of Shakespeare's "Sonnet 116" for an example of caesura.

> Let me not to the marriage of true minds
> Admit impediments. // Love is not love

Which alters when it alteration finds,

Note the period in the second line creating a caesura. When reading, there is not a pause until the caesura formed after the period in the middle of the second line. This continuation of the sentence onto the next line is called **enjambment**. The next pause does not appear until the end stopped line of the third line with the comma. The natural pauses created by punctuation and the meter shaped through the rising and falling of the syllables create poetic rhythm. Let's look at the three lines again, this time with stresses and metrical feet emphasized.

let ME / not TO / the MAR / riage OF / true MINDS
adMIT / imPED / iMENTS. // love IS / not LOVE
which AL / ters WHEN / it Al / terAT / ion FINDS,

Do you know what the above lines are written in? Since it starts with a stressed ,and is followed by an unstressed, foot of two syllables it is iambic with five metrical feet, making it pentameter. Now, a novice to poetry may ask why rhythm and meter is so important. In our contemporary time it is not as important as it was in the past. Looking at Shakespeare, it is important to know that he absolutely followed the rules of rhythm and meter, for if he did not, he would have been lambasted by readers and critics alike just as his contemporary John Donne, who broke away from these conventions, did and suffered for it in his own time. Thus, it is quite safe to assume that all of Shakespeare's sonnets followed iambic pentameter without question. Not knowing this, modern readers may be tempted to read the first line as "LET me NOT to the MARriage of TRUE MINDS," which is the natural rhythm of speaking now. This reading creates a softer, more contemplative tone about love.

Following the rules of iambic pentameter, however, the different meaning of the poem comes out. With the stress on "me" in the first line, there is a more inflected reaction throughout the rest of the poem, as if the speaker is defending himself. In the second line, the linking verb "is" is stressed along with the second "love." Compare "LOVE is NOT love" to "love IS not LOVE." The first sentence emphasizes that love is definitely not love. In the second line, it seems to be trying to say the opposite by emphasizing the linking verb and second "love."

TO AUTUMN

John Keats 1795-1821

1.
Season of mists and mellow fruitfulness,
    Close bosom-friend of the maturing sun;
Conspiring with him how to load and bless
    With fruit the vines that round the thatch-eves[1] run;
To bend with apples the mossed cottage-trees,
    And fill all fruit with ripeness to the core;
        To swell the gourd, and plump the hazel shells
    With a sweet kernel; to set budding more.
And still more, later flowers for the bees.
Until they think warm days will never cease,
    For Summer has o'er-brimmed their clammy cells[2].

2.
Who hath not seen thee[3] oft amid thy store?[4]
    Sometimes whoever seeks abroad may find
Thee sitting careless on a granary floor,
    Thy hair soft-lifted by the winnowing[5] wind;
Or on a half-reaped furrow sound asleep,
    Drowsed with the fume of poppies, while thy hook
        Spares the next swath[6] and all its twined flowers:
And sometimes like a gleaner[7] thou dost keep

1 thatch-eves: *n.* a roof made of straw
2 clammy cells: the honeycombed cells in a bee hive
3 thee: the speaker is addressing and personifying autumn
4 store: *n.* abundance
5 winnow: *v.* to remove the grain from the lighter chaff or covering
6 swath: *n.* the space left from the cut of a blade in tall grass

Steady thy laden head across a brook;
Or by a cyder-press,[8] with patient look.
Thou watchest the last oozings[9] hours by hours.

3.
Where are the songs of Spring? Ay; where are they?
Think not of them, thou hast thy music too,—
While barred clouds bloom the soft-dying day.
And touch the stubble-plains with rosy hue;
Then in a wailful[10] choir the small gnats mourn
Among the river sallows,[11] borne aloft
Or sinking as the light wind lives or dies;
And full-grown lambs loud bleat from hilly bourn;
Hedge-crickets sing; and now with treble soft
The red-breast[12] whistles from a garden-croft;[13]
And gathering swallows[14] twitter in the skies

---

7 gleaner: *n.* a person who gathers the grain after it has been cut
8 cyder-press: a machine that squeezes apples to make juice (cider)
9 oozing: *n.* the apple juice coming out of the press
10 wailful: *adj.* mournful; sad
11 sallow: *n.* a pussy willow
12 red-breast: *n.* a robin; bird
13 croft: *n.* a small strip of land next to a house for a garden
14 swallow: *n.* a small bird with long wings

CHARGE OF THE LIGHT BRIGADE

Lord Alfred Tennyson 1809-1892

Half a league,[1] half a league,
Half a league onward,
All in the valley of Death
Rode the six hundred:
"Forward, the Light Brigade![2]
Charge for the guns" he said:
Into the valley of Death
Rode the six hundred.

"Forward, the Light Brigade!"
Was there a man dismayed?
Not tho'[3] the soldiers knew
Some one had blundered:
Theirs not to make reply,
Theirs not to reason why,
Theirs but to do and die,
Into the valley of Death
Rode the six hundred.

Cannon to right of them,
Cannon to left of them,
Cannon in front of them
Volleyed[4] and thundered;
Stormed at with shot and shell,

1 league: *n.* old form meaning "five kilometers"
2 brigade: *n.* a large group of military troops
3 tho': *conj.* poetic form of "though"
4 volley: *v.* a number of cannon balls shot at the same time

Boldly they rode and well,
Into the jaws of Death,
Into the mouth of Hell
Rode the six hundred.

Flashed all their sabers[5] bare,
Flashed as they turned in air
Sabering[6] the gunners there,
Charging an army while
All the world wondered:
Plunged in the battery-smoke[7]
Right thro' the line they broke;
Cossack[8] and Russian
Reeled from the saber-stroke
Shattered and sundered.
Then they rode back, but not
Not the six hundred.

Cannon to right of them,
Cannon to left of them,
Cannon behind them
Volleyed and thundered;
Stormed at with shot and shell,
While horse and hero fell,
They that had fought so well
Came thro' the jaws of Death,
Back from the mouth of Hell,
All that was left of them,

5 saber: *n.* a slightly curved sword used by cavalry
6 saber: *v.* to stab someone with a saber
7 battery-smoke: *n.* the smoke that issues out of a cannon (battery)
8 Cossack: A southern Russian horseman

Left of six hundred.

When can their glory fade?
O the wild charge they made!
All the world wondered.
Honor the charge they made!
Honor the Light Brigade,
Noble six hundred!

THE LAMB

William Blake 1757-1827

Little Lamb, who made thee?
Dost thou know who made thee?
Gave thee life, and bid[1] thee feed,
By the stream and o'er the mead;[2]
Gave thee clothing of delight,
Softest clothing, woolly, bright;
Gave thee such a tender voice,
Making all the vales rejoice?
Little Lamb, who made thee?
Dost thou know who made thee?

Little Lamb, I'll tell thee,
Little Lamb, I'll tell thee.
He[3] is callèd by thy name,
For He calls Himself a Lamb.
He is meek, and He is mild;
He became a little child.
I a child, and thou a lamb,
We are called by His name.
Little Lamb, God bless thee!
Little Lamb, God bless thee!

1 bid: *v.* command
2 mead: *n.* meadow
3 He: Jesus Christ (the Lamb of God)

SHE WALKS IN BEAUTY

Lord George Gordon Byron 1788-1824

I

She walks in beauty—like the night
Of cloudless climes and starry skies,
And all that's best of dark and bright
Meet in her aspect and her eyes;
Thus mellowed to the tender light
Which heaven to gaudy day denies.

II

One shade the more, one ray the less,
Had half impaired the nameless grace
Which waves in every raven[1] tress[2]
Or softly lightens o'er[3] her face—
Where thoughts serenely sweet express
How pure, how dear their dwelling place.

III

And on that cheek and o'er that brow
So soft, so calm yet eloquent,
The smiles that win, the tints that glow
But tell of days in goodness spent
A mind at peace with all below,
A heart whose love is innocent.

1 raven: *adj.* black
2 tress: *n.* long lock of curly hair
3 o'er: over; used to turn a two syllable word into one

DULCE ET DECORUM EST[1]

Wilfred Owen 1893-1918

Bent double, like old beggars under sacks,
Knock-kneed,[2] coughing like hags,[3] we cursed through sludge,
Till on the haunting flares we turned our backs
And towards our distant rest[4] began to trudge.
Men marched asleep. Many had lost their boots
But limped on, blood-shod.[5] All went lame; all blind;
Drunk with fatigue; deaf even to the hoots[6]
Of tired, outstripped[7] Five-Nines[8] that dropped behind.

Gas! Gas! Quick, boys!–An ecstasy of fumbling,
Fitting the clumsy helmets[9] just in time;
But someone still was yelling out and stumbling
And flound'ring like a man in fire or lime... [10]
Dim, through the misty panes and thick green light,[11]
As under a green sea, I saw him drowning.

In all my dreams, before my helpless sight,
He plunges at me, guttering, choking, drowning.

---

1 Latin for "it is sweet and right;" a common saying during World War I

2 knock-kneed: *adj.* knees that are curved inward so they knock against each other when walking

3 hag: *n.* witch

4 distant rest: the camp away from the front lines where soldiers would recuperate during the fighting

5 blood-shod: *adj.* with bloody feet

6 hoot: (slang) the noise of shells flying through the air

7 outstripped: *adj.* to outrun something

8 Five-nines: (slang) 5.9 caliber explosive shell

9 helmet: what they used to call gasmasks during the war

10 lime: *n.* a type of poisonous chemical gas

11 the lenses (panes) of the gas masks were green colored

If in some smothering dreams you too could pace
Behind the wagon that we flung him in,
And watch the white eyes writhing in his face,
His hanging face, like a devil's sick of sin;
If you could hear, at every jolt, the blood
Come gargling from the froth-corrupted lungs,
Obscene as cancer, bitter as the cud[12]
Of vile, incurable sores on innocent tongues,–
My friend, you would not tell with such high zest
To children ardent[13] for some desperate glory,
The old Lie: *Dulce et decorum est*
Pro patria mori.[14]

12 cud: *n.* regurgitated grass that a cow constantly chews on
13 ardent: *adj.* eager
14 Latin for "it is sweet and right to die for your country"

ELEMENT *TEN*:

POETIC STRUCTURE

Introduction to Element *Ten*: Poetic Structure

Poetry, as we have studied so far, is not as easy as it seems. Poems are strong expressions of emotions, but to just emote on the page does not make a poem. Stringing rhymes together, even, does not constitute poetry. Even the seeming rambling style of free verse has some form of structure that poets are following to successful effect. Learning about poetic structure will increase your appreciation of poems and even help you compose your own. How a poem is organized is called **form,** and there are two types we will study: open form and closed form.

Free verse, poems that don't necessarily have conventional rhythm or rhyme, is a good example of **open form**, also referred to as free form. Open form does not mean form has been discarded, but it has actually been liberated and has given a poet a freer way of working ideas and structure. American poets like William Carlos Williams sought to create a more modern, a more real paradigm of American poetry that took scenes of the everyday and expressed them in a structure free from the prison of classical forms. A good example of open form poetry is Williams' "Red Wheel Barrow."

so much depends
upon

a red wheel
barrow

glazed with rain
water

beside the white
chickens.

Though this poem looks quite different, it does not use capital letters at the beginning of the lines, nor does it follow any set rhythm or meter. Any astute reader, however, may start to notice that this poem does have structure. Williams himself said: "No verse can be free, it must be governed by some measure, but not by the old measure. We have to return to a measure consonant with our time [...] a purely intuitive one which we feel but do not name."[1] The obvious structure is one sentence broken in to four equal stanzas. Each stanza has only two lines with exactly three words on the first and only one word on the second. The structure of the poem is also hinged upon the theme, which is mentioned in each stanza. Farming is dependent upon farming implements like the red wheel barrow, rain, and the animals on the farm such as chickens. Far from being a nonsense poem, it actually has a lot to say!

Opposed to open form is the **closed form** poem. With our understanding of rhythm and meter from the previous chapter, closed form poetry will be easier to analyze. Closed form means that a poem is fixed to certain number of lines and/or meter. For example, the most popular closed form poem is the **sonnet**, which originates from the Italian meaning "little song." The use of iambic pentameter in fourteen lines originates from these Italian songs as a cohesive poem that is divided into two types.

The first type is the **Petrarchan** or **Italian sonnet,** named after the great Italian writer Francesco Petrarch (1304-1374), which can be broken into two parts: an **octave** (8 lines) and a **sestet** (six lines). Let's look at John Milton's Petrarchan sonnet "When I Consider How My Light is Spent."

When I consider how my light is spent, *a*
  Ere[2] half my days in this dark world and wide, *b*

1 *Selected Essays*. New York: New Directions Publishing Corporation, 1954, page 339.

And that one talent which is death to hide *b*
Lodged with me useless, though my soul more bent *a*
To serve therewith my Maker,[3] and present *a*
My true account, lest He returning chide;[4] *b*
"Doth God exact day-labor, light denied?" *b*
I fondly ask. But Patience, to prevent *a*
That murmur, soon replies, "God doth not need *c*
Either man's work or His own gifts. Who best *d*
Bear His mild yoke,[5] they serve Him best. His state *e*
Is kingly: thousands at His bidding speed, *c*
And post o'er land and ocean without rest; *d*
They also serve who only stand and wait." *e*

To understand a sonnet, let's analyze its form. First, I have labeled the **rhyme scheme** to the side with *a, b, c,* and *d* rhymes. The rhyme scheme of *abbaabba* creates the octave, while this sonnet's sestet consists of *cde cde*. Other Petrarchan sonnets have various sestets with rhyme schemes of *ced ced*; or *cdd ccd*; or *cd cd cd*. The "theme" of the sonnet is usually set up in the octave, with the sestet introducing the **volta**, an unexpected or surprising thematic "twist," in line nine. Here, in the octet, the speaker contemplates how God will judge him. The third line mentions "that one talent which is death to hide," referencing the parable Jesus relates in the Bible about the talent. A talent is a coin that a servant is given by his master to make an increase. One servant, buries it; two others set out to invest the talent, but one loses it while the other actually increases his master's fortune. The servant who hid the talent is the one reprimanded by his master. The same can be said of us who hide our own talents or use them for overabundance. The speaker then asks a rhetorical question about God being a task master who demands work in exchange for "light" or spiritual illumination. The volta is God's unexpected response that fol-

2 Ere: *conj* before
3 Maker: God
4 chide: *v.* scold
5 yoke: *n.* a wooden frame that joins two animals together; a symbol of subjection

lows through the rest of the sestet. God reminds the speaker that He does not require work or need it, but blesses those who are willing to serve him with an open heart. It is not what we do; it is how we do it.

The other type of sonnet was made famous by Shakespeare, and, thus, the type he composed is called **Shakespearean** or **English sonnets**, and one of his more famous is "Sonnet 18."

Shall I compare thee to a summer's day? *a*
Thou art more lovely and more temperate: *b*
Rough winds do shake the darling buds of May, *a*
And summer's lease[6] hath all too short a date: *b*
Sometime too hot the eye of heaven[7] shines, *c*
And often is his gold complexion[8] dimmed, *d*
And every fair from fair sometime declines, *c*
By chance, or nature's changing course untrimmed: *d*
But thy eternal summer shall not fade, *e*
Nor lose possession of that fair thou ow'st,[9] *f*
Nor shall death brag thou wander'st in his shade, *e*
When in eternal lines to time thou grow'st, *f*
So long as men can breathe, or eyes can see, *g*
So long lives this, and this gives life to thee. *g*

The rhyme scheme of *abab* creates a **quatrain**, or four rhymed lines. A Shakespearean sonnet has three quatrains (*abab, cdcd, efef*), ending with a closed couplet with a rhyme scheme of *gg*. Traditional English sonnets usually set up a theme in the first two quatrains, and introduces the **volta** in the third. In the above sonnet, the speaker describes transitory nature of summer in the first two quatrains that eventually declines into fall. The volta comes in the third quatrain by shifting from the fleeting nature of summer to the eternal beauty of the woman

6 summer's lease: the season of summer
7 eye of heaven: the sun
8 complexion: face
9 ow'st: poetic form meaning 'owes'

he loves. The closed couplet usually expresses the speaker's emotional reaction to the previous quatrains. In this sonnet the poet glorifies in the fact that his beloved's beauty shall continue on forever as long as men can read the lines of this poem.

Another popular type of closed form poem is the **villanelle**, which has nineteen lines divided into six stanzas consisting of five tercets and a final quatrain. This is a rather strict form developed originally in France. One of the finest examples of a villanelle in the English language is "Do Not Go into That Good Night" by Dylan Thomas.

Do not go gentle into that good night, *a*
Old age should burn and rage at close of day; *b*
Rage, rage against the dying of the light. *a*

Though wise men at their end know dark is right, *a*
Because their words had forked no lightning they *b*
Do not go gentle into that good night. *a*

Good men, the last wave by, crying how bright *a*
Their frail deeds might have danced in a green bay, *b*
Rage, rage against the dying of the light. *a*

Wild men who caught and sang the sun in flight, *a*
And learn, too late, they grieved it on its way, *b*
Do not go gentle into that good night. *a*

Grave men, near death, who see with blinding sight *a*
Blind eyes could blaze like meteors and be gay, *b*
Rage, rage against the dying of the light. *a*

And you, my father, there on the sad height, *a*
Curse, bless me now with your fierce tears, I pray. *b*
Do not go gentle into that good night. *a*
Rage, rage against the dying of the light. *a*

Notice the villanelle rhyme scheme consists of only *a* and *b* rhymes, with the first and third line of each tercet rhyming followed by the second line rhyming in each of the following tercets. Also, the first line is repeated again in lines 6, 12, and 18, while the third line is additionally repeated in lines 9, 15, and 19. The repeated lines are found in the first tercet, only to be alternated in the following tercets and brought together again to create the final quatrain.

To better understand how stanzas are broken, remember that each line is formed into a stanza of which there are nine. The nine stanzas types with their accompanying rhyme scheme are listed as follows:

STANZA TYPE	NUMBER OF STANZA LINES	RHYME SCHEME
Couplet	two	aa
Tercet	three	rhyming varies
Quatrain (5 types, see below)	four	see below
Quintain	five	ababb (English Quintain)
Sextain (sestet)	six	ababab (traditional)
Chaucerian stanza (rhyme royal)	seven	ababbcc
Ottava Rima (octet or octave)	eight	abababcc
Spenserian Stanza	eight iambic pentameter + hexameter	ababbbcbbc
Fourteener	iambic heptameters as many as needed	rhyming varies

QUATRAIN TYPE	RHYME SCHEME
Ballad Quatrain	abcb
Heroic Quatrain	abab
Rhyme Enclosure	abba
Triple Quatrain	aaba
Double Couplet	aabb

I DREAMED IN A DREAM

Walt Whitman 1819-1892

I dreamed in a dream I saw a city invincible to the attacks of the
whole of the rest of the earth,
I dreamed that was the new city of Friends,
Nothing was greater there than the quality of robust love, it led
the rest,
It was seen every hour in the actions of the men of that city,
And in all their looks and words.

THE HOUSE ON THE HILL

Edwin Arlington Robinson 1869-1935

They are all gone away,
The house is shut and still,
There is nothing more to say.

Through broken walls and gray
The winds blow bleak and shrill:
They are all gone away.

Nor is there one today
To speak them good or ill:
There is nothing more to say.

Why is it then we stray
Around the sunken sill?
They are all gone away.

And our poor fancy-play
For them is wasted skill:
There is nothing more to say.

There is ruin and decay
In the House on the Hill
They are all gone away,
There is nothing more to say.

THE FEMALE VAGRANT

William Wordsworth 1788-1860

By Derwent's[1] side my Father's cottage stood,
(The Woman thus her artless story told)
One field, a flock, and what the neighboring flood
Supplied, to him were more than mines of gold.
Light was my sleep; my days in transport rolled:
With thoughtless joy I stretched along the shore
My father's nets, or from the mountain fold
Saw on the distant lake his twinkling oar
Or watched his lazy boat still less'ning more and more

My father was a good and pious man,
An honest man by honest parents bred,
And I believe that, soon as I began
To lisp, he made me kneel beside my bed,
And in his hearing there my prayers I said:
And afterwards, by my good father taught,
I read, and loved the books in which I read;
For books in every neighboring house I sought,
And nothing to my mind a sweeter pleasure brought.

Can I forget what charms did once adorn
My garden, stored with peas, and mint, and thyme,
And rose and lily for the sabbath morn?
The sabbath bells, and their delightful chime;
The gambols[2] and wild freaks[3] at shearing[4] time;

---

1 Derwent: a river in Cumbria, Northern England where Wordsworth was born and grew up
2 gambol: *n.* playfully running and jumping

My hen's rich nest through long grass scarce espied;[5]
The cowslip[6]-gathering at May's dewy prime;
The swans, that, when I sought the water-side,
From far to meet me came, spreading their snowy pride.

The staff I yet remember which upbore[7]
The bending body of my active sire;[8]
His seat beneath the honeyed sycamore
When the bees hummed, and chair by winter fire;
When market-morning came, the neat attire
With which, though bent on haste, myself I decked;[9]
My watchful dog, whose starts of furious ire,
When stranger passed, so often I have checked;
The red-breast[10] known for years, which at my casement[11] pecked.

The suns of twenty summers danced along,—
Ah! little marked, how fast they rolled away:
Then rose a stately hall our woods among,
And cottage after cottage owned its sway.
No joy to see a neighboring house, or stray
Through pastures not his own, the master took;
My Father dared his greedy wish gainsay;[12]
He loved his old hereditary nook,

3 freak: *n.* unpredictable prank or play
4 shearing time: the time of year that the wool is cut (sheared) from sheep
5 espy: *v.* to catch a glimpse of something
6 cowslip: *n.* a fragrant yellow flower
7 upbear: *v.* to sustain or support
8 sire: *n.* old form meaning 'father'
9 deck: *v.* to clothe
10 red-breast: *n.* a robin; a bird with red breast feathers
11 casement: *n.* window
12 gainsay: *v.* to contradict

And ill could I the thought of such sad parting brook.[13]

But when he had refused the proffered gold,
To cruel injuries he became a prey,
Sore traversed in whate'er he bought and sold:
His troubles grew upon him day by day,
Till all his substance fell into decay.
His little range of water[14] was denied;
All but the bed where his old body lay.
All, all was seized, and weeping, side by side,
We sought a home where we uninjured might abide.

13 brook: *v.* to suffer
14 little range of water: referring to the property on the Derwent River

SUMMER DAWN

William Morris 1834-1896

Pray but one prayer for me 'twixt thy closed lips,
Think but one thought of me up in the stars.
The summer night waneth,[1] the morning light slips,
Faint and grey 'twixt the leaves of the aspen, betwixt the cloud-bars[2]
That are patiently waiting there for the dawn:
Patient and colorless, though Heaven's gold
Waits to float through them along with the sun.
Far out in the meadows, above the young corn,
The heavy elms wait, and restless and cold
The uneasy wind rises; the roses are dun;[3]
Through the long twilight they pray for the dawn,
Round the lone house in the midst of the corn,
Speak but one word to me over the corn,
Over the tender, bowed locks of the corn.

1 waneth: *v.* old form meaning 'wanes'
2 cloud-bar: *n.* a long, narrow, unbroken line of clouds
3 dun: *adj.* a dull, grayish brown

MY LETTERS

Elizabeth Browning 1806-1861

My letters! all dead paper, mute and white!
And yet they seem alive and quivering
Against my tremulous hands which loose the string
And let them drop down on my knee tonight.
This said—he wished to have me in his sight
Once, as a friend: this fixed a day in spring
To come and touch my hand. . . a simple thing,
Yes I wept for it—this . . . the paper's light. . .
Said, Dear, I love thee; and I sank and quailed[1]
As if God's future thundered on my past.
This said, I am thine—and so its ink has paled
With lying at my heart that beat too fast.
And this . . . O Love, thy words have ill availed
If, what this said, I dared repeat at last!

1 quail: *v.* to lose courage in the face of danger

ODE TO THE WEST WIND

Percy Bysshe Shelley 1792-1822

I

O wild West Wind, thou breath of Autumn's being,
Thou, from whose unseen presence the leaves dead
Are driven, like ghosts from an enchanter fleeing,

Yellow, and black, and pale, and hectic red,
Pestilence-stricken multitudes: O thou,
Who chariotest[1] to their dark wintry bed

The wingèd seeds, where they lie cold and low,
Each like a corpse within its grave, until
Thine azure[2] sister of the Spring shall blow

Her clarion[3] o'er the dreaming earth, and fill
(Driving sweet buds like flocks to feed in air)
With living hues and odors plain and hill:

Wild Spirit, which art moving everywhere;
Destroyer and Preserver; hear, O hear!

II

Thou on whose stream, 'mid the steep sky's commotion,
Loose clouds like Earth's decaying leaves are shed,
Shook from the tangled boughs of Heaven and Ocean,

---

1 chariotest: *v.* to carry
2 azure: *adj.* sky blue
3 clarion: *n.* a curved trumpet

Angels of rain and lightning: there are spread
On the blue surface of thine airy surge,
Like the bright hair uplifted from the head

Of some fierce Maenad,[4] even from the dim verge
Of the horizon to the zenith's height,
The locks of the approaching storm. Thou dirge

Of the dying year, to which this closing night
Will be the dome of a vast sepulcher
Vaulted with all thy congregated might

Of vapors, from whose solid atmosphere
Black rain, and fire, and hail will burst: O hear!

III

Thou who didst waken from his summer dreams
The blue Mediterranean, where he lay,
Lulled by the coil of his crystalline streams,

Beside a pumice[5] isle in Baiae's[6] bay,
And saw in sleep old palaces and towers
Quivering within the wave's intenser day,

All overgrown with azure moss and flowers
So sweet, the sense faints picturing them! Thou
For whose path the Atlantic's level powers

4 Maenad: the mad female worshippers of Dionysus, the Greek god of wine and fertility
5 pumice: *n.* a porous stone of volcanic glass
6 Baiae: an ancient resort city in SW Italy

Cleave themselves into chasms, while far below
The sea-blooms and the oozy woods which wear
The sapless foliage of the ocean, know

Thy voice, and suddenly grow grey with fear,
And tremble and despoil themselves: O hear!

IV
If I were a dead leaf thou mightest bear;
If I were a swift cloud to fly with thee;
A wave to pant beneath thy power, and share

The impulse of thy strength, only less free
Than thou, O Uncontrollable! If even
I were as in my boyhood, and could be

The comrade of thy wanderings over Heaven,
As then, when to outstrip thy skiey[7] speed
Scarce seemed a vision; I would ne'er have striven

As thus with thee in prayer in my sore need.
Oh! lift me as a wave, a leaf, a cloud!
I fall upon the thorns of life! I bleed!

A heavy weight of hours has chained and bowed
One too like thee: tameless, and swift, and proud.

V
Make me thy lyre,[8] even as the forest is:

7 skiey: *adj.* of the sky
8 lyre: *n.* a musical strumming instrument

What if my leaves are falling like its own!
The tumult of thy mighty harmonies

Will take from both a deep, autumnal tone,
Sweet though in sadness. Be thou, Spirit fierce,
My spirit! Be thou me, impetuous[9] one!

Drive my dead thoughts over the universe
Like withered leaves to quicken a new birth!
And, by the incantation of this verse,

Scatter, as from an unextinguished hearth
Ashes and sparks, my words among mankind!
Be through my lips to unawakened Earth

The trumpet of a prophecy! O Wind,
If Winter comes, can Spring be far behind?

---

9 impetuous: *adj.* doing rash action

ELEMENT *ELEVEN*:

THE SOUND OF POETRY

Introduction to Element Eleven: The Sound of Poetry

Poetry has a distinct sound that separates it from prose. We often think of poetry as rhyming, and, indeed, most of the classical forms of poetry do rhyme as are found in this anthology; however, the modern movement of the early 20th century moved poetry into non-rhyming verse, which has various forms, such as free verse and blank verse. Without rhyme, poets rely on other techniques, such as syntax, to give shape to their poems. Consider this free verse poem "The Young House Wife" by William Carlos Williams.

At ten A.M. the young housewife
moves about in negligee[1] behind
the wooden walls of her husband's house.
I pass solitary in my car.

Then again she comes to the curb
to call the ice-man, fish-man, and stands
shy, uncorseted,[2] tucking in
stray ends of hair, and I compare her
to a fallen leaf.

The noiseless wheels of my car
rush with a crackling sound over
dried leaves as I bow and pass smiling.

True **free verse** strays as far from tradition as possible by creating

1 negligee: *n.* a light, revealing nightgown

2 uncorseted: a corset is a tight fitting garment meant to make a woman look slim; it connotes being under male control; being uncorseted suggests being free of her husband's influence

imagery and emotion instead of strict poetic formulas. In the above poem, the poet is "painting" a picture of a lonely housewife by avoiding traditional techniques of rhyme, rhythm, and meter. Notice that the poem utilizes syntax to create poetic form instead of rhyme. Instead of the standard layout to create rhythm, Williams creates his own pauses by creating short stanzas and lines. If we look at the third line in the second stanza we can see the effect of non-traditional line breaking. The young housewife goes to the curb to talk to different deliverymen, being shy and uncorseted. When the speaker mention her "tucking in" something, we automatically assume she is going to tuck in an article of clothing, but the next line reveals it is her hair. We now realize that she is more concerned about her looks than we were led to believe.

Let's now look at Robert Frost's "Mending Wall" as another example of free verse.

> Something there is that doesn't love a wall,
> That sends the frozen-ground-swell under it,
> And spills the upper boulders in the sun,
> And makes gaps even two can pass abreast.
> The work of hunters is another thing:
> I have come after them and made repair
> Where they have left not one stone on a stone,
> But they would have the rabbit out of hiding,
> To please the yelping dogs. The gaps I mean,
> No one has seen them made or heard them made,
> But at spring mending-time we find them there.

The lines do not rhyme, but they do still maintain a regular structure of iambic pentameter, which also requires ten syllables per line for the most part. Line 8 does have eleven syllables to force the rhythm to stumble, thus, to force the reader to pay extra attention to what is being said, which is highlighted in the following line by putting a period in the middle, creating caesura. Free verse has been as popular as rhyming poetry in that most epic poetry and plays utilize it. For example, John Milton's Paradise Lost and most of Shakespeare's plays have free verse.

Rhymed poetry, however, is so much more difficult to produce than most readers think. In fact, Robert Frost visited students at Milton Academy in 1935 and said, "I had soon write free verse as play tennis with the net down."[3] There is some truth to this statement. Rhyming adds an element of challenge, but it adds a whole new dimension to understanding the poem. Poets not only have to match the final consonant and vowel sounds of two or more words, they have to decide where to place the corresponding rhymes. When the same ending sounds occur at the end of lines, they are called **end rhymes**, and when they are found within the lines, they are called **internal rhymes.**

End rhymes are easy to find and are the most popular, as found in Robert Herrick's "Upon Julia's Clothes."

> Whenas[4] in silks my Julia g**oes**,
> Then, then, methinks, how sweetly fl**ows**
> That liquefaction[5] of her cl**othes**.
>
> Next, when I cast mine eyes, and s**ee**
> That brave vibration, each way fr**ee**,
> O, how that glittering taketh m**e**!

Each stanza has three end rhymes that are exact—*goes, flows, clothes,* for example. Such rhymes create an allusion of repetition without boring the reader. End rhymes are also excellent for giving closure to a poem, giving closure to the reading experience. This is especially used well in the **closed couplet**. Shakespeare used the couplet with utmost satisfaction in his sonnets, as in "So long as men can breathe, or eyes can s**ee**, / So long lives this, and this gives life to th**ee**" found at the end of "Sonnet 18".

Internal rhyme is another devise that is common in poetry but may not be noticed as much by first time readers. One of the best

3 Robert Frost: Collected Poems, Prose, and Plays. Library of America, page 809
4 whenas: (conj) old form meaning 'when'
5 liquefaction: *n.* the state of being liquid or looking like liquid

poems to use internal rhyme is "The Raven" by Edgar Allan Poe.

> Once upon a midnight **dreary**, while I pondered, weak and **weary**,
> Over many a quaint and curious volume of forgotten *lore*,
> While I nodded, nearly **napping**, suddenly there came a **tap-ping**,
> As of someone gently **rapping, rapping** at my chamber *door*.
> "'Tis some visitor," I muttered, "**tapping** at my chamber *door* —
> Only this, and nothing *more*."

The bolded words indicate the internal rhyme, while the italicized words are the end rhymes. What makes Poe's poem all the more memorable is that he was able to use both end and internal rhyme to his advantage.

Rhymes are not as straight forward as we may originally think. As you may have noticed, not all rhymes sound perfectly the same, or even have the same stress. There are several forms of general rhymes that we should know before we proceed: alliteration, assonance, consonance, half rhyme, masculine and feminine rhymes, sight rhyme, slant rhyme, and triple rhyme. First, **alliteration** is matching the first consonants of words and can be found throughout a line. Most popular with Old English poetry, it survives to this day. An example is found in Poe's "The Raven" when he writes, "**w**eak and **w**eary", "**q**uaint and **c**urious", and "While I **n**odded, **n**early **n**apping."

Another rhyme is **assonance**, where the vowels are matched instead of the consonants, as in Lord Alfred Tennyson's "The Lotus-Eaters."

> **A**nd round **a**bout the keel[6] with f*a*ces p*a*le,
> Dark f*a*ces p*a*le ag*ai*nst that rosy fl*a*me,
> The m**i**ld-**eye**d melancholy Lotos-eaters c*a*me.

Assonance is achieved with the long "a" sound in all three lines. There is also assonance found in the short "a" sound in the first line and

6 keel: *n.* boat or ship

the long "i" in the third line.

Next, we have **consonance**, which matches any consonants in the line as opposed to just the initial consonants of alliteration. Further into Poe's "The Raven" consonance is beautifully written, "And the **s**ilken **s**ad un**c**ertain ru**st**ling of each p*ur*ple c*ur*tain." Notice the assonance of the "ur" sound at the end of the line as well.

The fourth type usually created as the result of consonance is the **half** (or sprung) **rhyme**, where the final consonants are matched at the end of the lines, but the vowels do not. William Butler Yeats wrote many of his poems in half rhyme, such as "Lines Written in Dejection."

> When have I last looked o**n**
> The round green eyes and the long wavering bodies
> Of the dark leopards of the moo**n**?
> All the wild witches, those most noble ladies,
> For all their broom-sticks and their tears,
> Their angry tears, are go**ne**.
> The holy centaurs[7] of the hills are vanished;
> I have nothing but the embittered su**n**;
> Banished heroic mother moon and vanished,
> And now that I have come to fifty years
> I must endure the timid su**n**.

Notice that "on" and "moon" both end with the same vowel and consonant, but they vowels are different — short vowel and long vowel. "Gone" and "sun" have different vowels, but the same consonant ending while the other lines have the more traditional end rhyme usage.

A **masculine rhyme**, or single rhyme, has the two or more words that rhyme through the final syllables, which are stressed or which are only one syllable. Most of the rhymes we have been looking at are masculine rhymes, as can be seen in John Donne's "Lecture Upon a Shadow."

7 centaur: *n.* a mythical creature with the upper body of a man and lower body of a horse

Stand still, and I will read to **thee**
A lecture, love, in Love's philoso**phy**.
These three hours that we have **spent**
Walking here, two shadows **went**
Along with us, which we ourselves pro**duced**.
But now the sun is just above our **head**,
We do those shadows **tread**,
And to brave clearness all things are re**duced**.

A **feminine rhyme** has two syllables that rhyme; therefore, is also known as a double rhyme. The first syllable is stressed with an unstressed consonant. Robert Frost loved to write with both masculine and feminine rhymes, as can be seen in his poem "Nothing Gold Can Stay."

Nature's first green is g**old**,
Her hardest hue to h**old**.
Her early leaf's a fl*ower*;
But only so an h*our*.
Then leaf subsides to l**eaf**.
So Eden[8] sank to gr**ief**,
So dawn goes down to d**ay**.
Nothing gold can st**ay**.

Notice that the last syllables in bold are masculine rhymes while "flower" and "hour," with two rhyming syllables are feminine. You may have noticed that "today" is split into two words, "to day." This is not a typing error; it is to maintain his masculine rhyme scheme.

Frost also used feminine rhyme to call attention to certain words or ideas. This is made obvious in the last stanza of his poem "Reluctance," where he interspersed feminine rhymes with masculine endings:

Out through the fields and the woods
And over the walls I have w**ended**;[9]

8 Eden: the Biblical paradise where the first man and woman, Adam and Eve, were created and were later cast out of for eating the forbidden fruit

I have climbed the hills of view
And looked at the world, and desc**ended**;
I have come by the highway home,
And lo, it is **ended**.

The leaves are all dead on the ground,
Save those that the oak is k**eeping**
To ravel them one by one
And let them go scraping and cr**eeping**
Out over the crusted snow,
When others are **sleeping**.

And the dead leaves lie huddled and still,
No longer blown hither and th**ither**;
The last lone aster[10] is gone;
The flowers of the witch-hazel w**ither**;
The heart is still aching to seek,
But the feet question 'Wh**ither**?'[11]

Ah, when to the heart of man
Was it ever less than a tr**eason**
To go with the drift of things,
To yield with a grace to r**eason**,
And bow and accept the end
Of a love or a s**eason**?

Notice the bold words are feminine rhymes following masculine ending lines. If we look closely at the last stanza, Frost purposefully accented "season" on the second to last syllable so that it would be a feminine rhyme. Feminine rhymes are more difficult to use than masculine rhymes. How many words actually rhyme with season? Frost would take words like "treason" and "reason" just to use them for their feminine rhyme, and then separate them with masculine endings that didn't rhyme but had one syllable. Notice that he offsets the feminine rhyme lines to accentuate the difference between his mas-

9 wend: *v.* to go
10 aster: *n.* a flower similar to a sunflower
11 whither: *adv.* to what place?

culine ending and feminine rhyme.

A seventh type of rhyme **sight rhymes** cause some confusion for second language learners because they have the same spelling, but the pronunciation is a little off or completely different. A good example of a sight rhyme is found in the second stanza of "The Snail" by William Cowper.

> Wherever he dwells, he dwells al**one**,
> Except himself, has chattels[12] n**one**,
> Well satisfied to be his own
> Whole treasure.

Though the spelling of the final syllables are the same in the first two lines, "alone" has a long vowel, whereas "none" has a short vowel. These should not be forced to rhyme, but pronounced as is. Robert Herrick used imperfect rhymes frequently in his poetry such as in "His Return to London." "Ravished in spirit, I come, nay more I fl**y** / To thee, blest place of my nativit**y**!" Again do not force the rhyme, but let it be pronounced as is natural.

Eighth, **slant rhymes** are forms of half rhymes, and are important to know. They are created through either assonance or consonance, which creates a sound close enough to another's, but it is still not quite a full rhyme. Let's look at Dickinson's poem "The Difference Between Despair" for a good example of a slant rhyme:

> The Mind is Smooth—no Motion—
> Contented as the E**ye**
> Upon the Forehead of a Bust—
> That knows—it cannot s**ee**.

"Eye" and "see" do not perfectly rhyme, but they do create a slant rhyme through the similarity of end vowels. Such a rhyme is evocative, even disconcerting; the slant on the rhyme matches the slant on the theme. The eye on the "forehead of a bust" that Dickenson mentions

12 chattel: *n.* belongings

could reference a statue of a Cyclops, whose sight is already hindered by having just one eye. The tragedy of the final two lines is that its hindered sight is completely blinded as a statue.

The final type, a **triple rhyme**, is where two words with the same stressed syllable are followed by two unstressed syllables. Lord Byron used triple rhyme rather well throughout his long satirical poem *Don Juan*. A good example as any is found in stanza 20 of Canto One:

Now Donna[13] Inez had, with all her m*erit*,
    A great opinion of her own good qu**alities;**
Neglect, indeed, requires a saint to b*ear it*,
    And such, indeed, she was in her mor**alities**;
But then she had a devil of a sp*irit*,
    And sometimes mixed up fancies with re**alities**,
And let few opportunities escape
Of getting her liege lord into a scrape.

As can be imagined, in order to get these three triple rhymes, Lord Byron had to choose them before he wrote the verse and then match up his ideas to fit. Notice the feminine rhymes in *italics*. With an understanding of the different types of rhyme, we can get a better appreciation as to how difficult it can actually be to construct a poem of absolute beauty.

Let's now take a final look at a poem by Gerard Manley Hopkins that incorporates as many of our rhymes as possible.

SPRING AND FALL
To a Young Child

M*árgár*et, *ar*e you griéving
Over Goldengrove[14] unleaving?
Leaves, **l**ike the things of man, you
With your **f**resh thoughts care **f**or, can you?

alliteration / consonance
assonance
feminine rhymes

13 donna: a Spanish title equivalent to Mrs.; don is equivalent to Mr.
14 Golden Grove: an Elizabethan period manor that was prominent in Hopkins's time

Ah! as the heart grows older
It will come to such sights colder[15]
By and by, nor spare a sigh
Though worlds of wanwood[16] leafmeal[17] lie;
And yet you will weep and know why.
Now no matter, child, the name:
Sorrow's springs are the same.
Nor mouth had, no nor mind, expressed
What héart héard of, ghóst guéssed:
It is the blight man was born for,
It is Margaret you mourn for.

masculine rhymes

Because every line rhymes, every ending syllable is considered an ending rhyme. Hopkins does use an **internal rhyme** in line 7 when he writes, "By and by, nor spare a *sigh*."

15 colder: in this case meaning 'less emotion'
16 wanwood: probably meaning 'a dark forest'
17 leafmeal: another form meaning "piecemeal'; all the leaves of the forest have fallen

A NOISELESS PATIENT SPIDER

Walt Whitman 1819-1892

A noiseless, patient spider,
I marked, where, on a little promontory, it stood, isolated;
Marked how, to explore the vacant, vast surrounding,
It launched forth filament, filament, filament, out of itself;
Ever unreeling them—ever tirelessly speeding them.

And you, O my Soul, where you stand,
Surrounded, surrounded, in measureless oceans of space,
Ceaselessly musing, venturing, throwing,—seeking the spheres,
to
connect them;
Till the bridge you will need, be form'd—till the ductile anchor
hold;
Till the gossamer thread you fling, catch somewhere, O my Soul.

ON JULIA'S VOICE

Robert Herrick 1591-1674

So smooth, so sweet, so silv'ry is thy voice,
As, could they hear, the Damned would make no noise,
But listen to thee (walking in thy chamber)
Melting melodious words to Lutes[1] of Amber.[2]

1 lute: *n.* a pear-shaped stringed instrument similar to a guitar
2 amber: *n.* a yellowish-brown color, often associated with luxury or richness

DOVER BEACH[1]

Matthew Arnold 1822-1888

The sea is calm to-night.
The tide is full, the moon lies fair
Upon the straits;—on the French coast the light
Gleams and is gone; the cliffs of England stand,
Glimmering and vast, out in the tranquil bay.
Come to the window, sweet is the night-air!
Only, from the long line of spray
Where the sea meets the moon-blanched[2] land,
Listen! you hear the grating roar
Of pebbles which the waves draw back, and fling,
At their return, up the high strand,[3]
Begin, and cease, and then again begin,
With tremulous[4] cadence slow, and bring
The eternal note of sadness in.

Sophocles[5] long ago
Heard it on the Aegean,[6] and it brought
Into his mind the turbid[7] ebb and flow
Of human misery; we
Find also in the sound a thought,
Hearing it by this distant northern sea.

---

1 Dover Beach: An English port that sits at the narrowest point between England and France
2 moon-blanched: *adj.* pale under the moon
3 strand: *n.* a beach or shore
4 tremulous: *adj.* vibrating
5 Sophocles: a Greek dramatist of 5th century B.C.
6 Aegean: the sea surrounding Greece
7 turbid: *adj.* shadowy

The Sea of Faith[8]
Was once, too, at the full, and round earth's shore
Lay like the folds of a bright girdle furled.
But now I only hear
Its melancholy, long, withdrawing roar,
Retreating, to the breath
Of the night-wind, down the vast edges drear
And naked shingles[9] of the world.

Ah, love, let us be true
To one another! for the world, which seems
To lie before us like a land of dreams,
So various, so beautiful, so new,
Hath really neither joy, nor love, nor light,
Nor certitude, nor peace, nor help for pain;
And we are here as on a darkling plain
Swept with confused alarms of struggle and flight,
Where ignorant armies clash by night.

8 Sea of Faith: a metaphor for the religious beliefs of the world
9 shingle: *n.* a beach of round smooth pebbles

LEDA AND THE SWAN[1]

William Butler Yeats 1865-1935

A sudden blow: the great wings beating still
Above the staggering girl, her thighs caressed
By the dark webs,[2] her nape caught in his bill,
He holds her helpless breast upon his breast.

How can those terrified vague fingers push
The feathered glory from her loosening thighs?
And how can body, laid in that white rush,
But feel the strange heart beating where it lies?

A shudder in the loins engenders[3] there
The broken wall, the burning roof and tower
And Agamemnon dead.[4]
Being so caught up,
So mastered by the brute blood of the air,
Did she put on his knowledge with his power
Before the indifferent beak could let her drop?

1 In Greek mythology, Zeus fell in love with the beauty of Leda and appeared before her in the shape of a swan and raped her. She gave birth to Helen, whose beauty started the Trojan War.

2 webs: the webbed feet of the swan

3 engenders: *v.* to be produced or caused

4 The broken wall...Agamemnon dead: a reference to the Trojan war that started with the infidelity of Leda's daughter Helen.

SONG

Amelia Opie 1769-1853

I am wearing away like the snow in the sun,
I am wearing away from the pain in my heart;
But ne'er shall he know, who my peace has undone,
How bitter, how lasting, how deep is my smart.

I know he would pity-so kind is his soul,
To him my affliction would agony be;
But never, while I can my feelings control,
The youth whom I love shall know sorrow through me.

Though longing to weep, in his presence I'll smile,
Call the flush of my cheek the pure crimson of health;
His fears for my peace by my song I'll beguile,
Nor venture to gaze on his eyes but by stealth.

For conscious I am, by my glance is exprest[1]
The passion that faithful as hopeless will be,
And he, whom, alas! I can ne'er render blest,
Shall never, no never, know sorrow through me.

1 exprest: expressed

ELEMENT *TWELVE*:
POETIC TYPES

Introduction to Element Twelve: Poetic Types

Poetry is as complex and engaging as fiction. In fact, there are two types of poetry that we need to understand: lyrical and narrative. If you like songs and singing, then you best turn to lyrical poetry. If you are looking for a good action story, then narrative poetry is for you. Both types of poetry can be divided into smaller units. Let's take a closer look at each of these two types and subdivisions.

We will not spend too much time with lyrical poetry, since it is what most of the poems found in this text are, but it is important to understand the difference between lyrical and narrative. **Lyrical poetry** is less concerned about plot and action; thus, it focuses on song and emotion. These poems are briefer than narrative and center on the thoughts and emotions of the speaker rather than on a protagonist. It is also more difficult to decipher than narrative, which is why we have focused on various elements of poetry to help understand the overall meaning of the lyrical poem. The rhythm and meter creates the songlike quality of the poem. Narrative poems have ballads that are also set to song, but they contain plot and action; whereas, lyrical poems focus on emotion. Because of the brief intensity of emotion displayed in lyrical poetry, it is has outlasted narrative poetry into the 21st century. It is still favored in poetic form as well as in all forms of songs, including rap music. Since lyrical poetry has been explored in more detail in "Element 10: Poetic Structure," let's move on to the second type of poetry.

Narrative poetry is easy to identify because it is poetry with a plot. It is an old art form and was around before movies, books, and even writing. It was used by early societies to preserve wisdom, myths, and also to entertain. The longest type of narrative is called an **epic**, Greek for word, story, or poem. Beginning as an oral form, epic poems were serious in tone and celebrated the lives of the gods and the exploits of heroes. The creation of the world, the origins of civilization, along with religious beliefs and ideologies are often found in ancient epic poems. Unfortunately, since epics abounded before the advent of writing, most are lost to the modern ear. The earliest work of literature is the epic poem Gilgamesh (originating in 2150-2000 BC, but the earliest known written table is around 1300-1000 BC). Some scholars state that these earlier epics highly influenced Homer (9th century BC) in Greece, who is famous for *The Iliad* and *The Odyssey*. Since these epics portray lofty ideals, the writing is as grand and serious as the subject matter. Following the ideals of Greek epics were the Romans (Virgil's *Aeneid* 1st century BC), the Italians (Dante's *Divine Comedy* 13th Century AD), the English (Milton's *Paradise Lost* 17th Century AD), and into modern times, the Americans (Henry Wadsworth Longfellow's *Hiawatha* 19th Century).

Let's look at some superb examples of epics through the ages. One of the most important English epics is Beowulf, it is not known when it was actually set to paper (between 8th to 11th century AD); it was written in Old English, which is as foreign to English as German is. Here is the lofty beginning of the epic that introduces the lineage and character of the hero Beowulf.

> Lo, praise of the prowess of people-kings
> of spear-armed Danes, in days long sped,
> we have heard, and what honor the athelings[1] won!
> Oft Scyld the Scefing[2] from squadroned[3] foes,
> from many a tribe, the mead-bench[4] tore,
> awing the earls. Since erst[5] he lay
> friendless, a foundling,[6] fate repaid him:
> for he waxed under welkin,[7] in wealth he throve,

1 atheling: Old English word meaning 'prince'
2 Scyld the Scefing: Legendary progenitor of the Danish royal line
3 squadron: *v.* to form a squadron
4 mead-bench: a table where the warrior class would drink mead (a type of beer)
5 erst: *adv.* old form meaning 'formerly'
6 foundling: *n.* an abandoned child

till before him the folk, both far and near,
who house by the whale-path,[8] heard his mandate,
gave him gifts: a good king he!
To him an heir was afterward born,
a son in his halls, whom heaven sent
to favor the folk, feeling their woe
that erst they had lacked an earl for leader
so long a while; the Lord endowed him,
the Wielder of Wonder, with world's renown.

Famed was this Beowulf: far flew the boast of him,
son of Scyld, in the Scandian[9] lands.
So becomes it a youth to quit him well
with his father's friends, by fee and gift,
that to aid him, aged, in after days,
come warriors willing, should war draw nigh,
liegemen[10] loyal: by lauded deeds
shall an earl have honor in every clan.
Forth he fared at the fated moment,
sturdy Scyld to the shelter of God.

Such a beginning suggests the hero's beginnings are far from normal, and Beowulf is elevated to a plane equal to that of the mightiest kings. Compare this opening with a more modern form of English by way of Milton's Paradise Lost, which copies the classical mode of invoking the muse and setting the story in a vast landscape, such as Heaven.

Of Man's first disobedience, and the fruit
Of that forbidden tree whose mortal taste
Brought death into the World, and all our woe,
With loss of Eden, till one greater Man

Restore us, and regain the blissful seat,
Sing, Heavenly Muse, that, on the secret top

7 welkin: from the Old English form meaning 'sky'
8 whale-path: *n.* sea
9 Scandian: another form for 'Scandinavian'
10 liegeman: *n.* a vassal or subject

Of Oreb,[11] or of Sinai,[12] didst inspire
That shepherd[13] who first taught the chosen seed
In the beginning how the heavens and earth

Rose out of Chaos:

Here the poet, in classical form, invokes the muse to aid him in retelling the tale of Adam and Eve's fall from the Garden of Eden, and wishes to be as inspired as Moses (the shepherd of line 8), who received on Sinai Mountain the writings about the creation of the world recorded in Genesis. He goes on to tell of the epic war in heaven between Jehovah and Satan and how it led to the fall of Adam.

The second type of narrative, and by far the most popular, is the **ballad**. Often set to music and sung by medieval minstrels, ballads were also passed on orally and not until poets wrote them down do we have a definitive record of them. There are records referencing popular ballads of *Robin Hood* in the 14th century, and the 15th century abounded with printed ballads, which shows evidence of the popular appeal of this narrative form. It could be argued that medieval ballads were an early form of pop music. A famous traditional ballad is "Kemp Owyne" of which a fragment is presented below:

Her mother died when she was young,
Which gave her cause to make great moan;
Her father married the worst woman
That ever lived in Christendom.
She served her with foot and hand,
In every thing that she could dee,[14]
Till once, in an unlucky time,
She threw her in over Craigy's sea.
Says, 'Lie you there, dove Isabel,
And all my sorrows lie with thee;

11 Oreb: and alternative spelling of Horeb; also known as Sinai

12 Sinai: The mountain in Egypt where Moses talked with God and received the Ten Commandments

13 shepherd: referring to the great prophet Moses who had humble beginnings as a shepherd

14 dee: *v.* Old English form meaning 'do'

Till Kemp Owyne come over the sea,
And borrow you with kisses three,
Let all the world do what they will,
Oh borrowed shall you never be!'
Her breath grew strange, her hair grew long,
And twisted thrice about the tree,
And all the people, far and near,
Thought that a savage beast was she.

The rhythm and rhyme of this ballad has a sing-song quality to it. Any ballad you read could easily be set to music. You may have also noticed that these early ballads have a fairy-tale sensibility to them. In the above section, we have a fair maiden whose mother has died and whose father has remarried a horrible woman. This evil step-mother demands slave service of her step-daughter, and is eventually cursed as an ugly beast until the time Kemp Owyne comes and kisses her to set her free.

What sets the ballad apart from the epic is that it is often set locally instead of over many nations or over great periods of time and space; and though the story does offer extraordinary episodes of heroism, they are written in simple, direct language with little care about characterization. Like the epic, ballad lines or stanzas are often repeated, but the action occurs immediately and often with surprise endings, unlike the drawn out battles of the epics which seem to go on for pages and pages.

Out of the popularity of the often base traditional ballads, were the **literary ballads** born. Made especially popular in the Romantic period of the 19th century, these ballads imitated the original forms as listed in the previous paragraph, but with a more conscious effort to invoke poetic style and techniques. Scotland is famous for literary ballads with poems by Robert Burns, while in England ballads by Samuel Taylor Coleridge and William Wordsworth made such a style mythic. Coleridge's "Rime of the Ancient Mariner" is by far one of the most popular. Though it is too long to print in this text, a sample is given below. After a ship is stranded in the Antarctic, an albatross guides the ship and crew to safer waters only to be shot by the Mariner.

By killing such a good omen, the ship and crew are cursed by a dead calm, water and weather so tranquil that the ship is stranded once again. Coleridge records the beginning of the cursed ordeal as follows:

> The fair breeze blew, the white foam flew,
> The furrow[15] followed free;
> We were the first that ever burst
> Into that silent sea.
>
> The ship hath been suddenly becalmed.
> Down dropt the breeze, the sails dropt down,
> 'Twas sad as sad could be ;
> And we did speak only to break
> The silence of the sea!
>
> All in a hot and copper sky,
> The bloody Sun, at noon,
> Right up above the mast did stand,
> No bigger than the Moon.
>
> Day after day, day after day,
> We stuck, nor breath nor motion;
> As idle as a painted ship
> Upon a painted ocean.
>
> And the Albatross begins to be avenged.
> Water, water, every where,
> And all the boards did shrink ;
> Water, water, every where,
> Nor any drop to drink.

The third type of narrative poetry is **romance**. Popular in the medieval period, the subject matter often dealt with knights and Arthurian legends. These poems deal with acts of chivalry, knights fighting dragons and monsters to acquire great treasure or to rescue damsels in distress. Other romances often deal with mythological stories as

15 furrow: *n.* the indentation in the ocean created by the hull of the ship

well. Lord Alfred Tennyson's *Idylls of the King*, a retelling of the legend of King Arthur, is a good example of narrative romance. Here, written in poetic form, is the legendary bestowal of Excalibur.

> 'And there I saw mage Merlin, whose vast wit
> And hundred winters are but as the hands
> Of loyal vassals toiling for their liege.
> 'And near him stood the Lady of the Lake,
> Who knows a subtler magic than his own —
> Clothed in white samite,[16] mystic, wonderful.
> She gave the King his huge cross-hilted sword,
> Whereby to drive the heathen out: a mist
> Of incense curled about her, and her face
> Wellnigh[17] was hidden in the minster gloom;
> But there was heard among the holy hymns
> A voice as of the waters, for she dwells
> Down in a deep; calm, whatsoever storms
> May shake the world, and when the surface rolls,
> Hath power to walk the waters like our Lord.
>
> 'There likewise I beheld Excalibur
> Before him at his crowning borne, the sword
> That rose from out the bosom of the lake,
> And Arthur rowed across and took it — rich
> With jewels, elfin Urim,[18] on the hilt,
> Bewildering heart and eye — the blade so bright
> That men are blinded by it — on one side

Because of its magical and often fantastical qualities, romance as a poetic narrative form has waned in favor, though it is still kept alive in fiction, especially fantasy fiction made popular by J.R.R. Tolkien's *The Lord of the Rings*.

16 samite: *n.* a silk fabric interwoven with gold popular in the middle ages

17 Wellnigh: *adv.* almost

18 Urim: a precious stone mentioned in the Old Testament through which the high priest received direct revelation from God; by combining pagan 'elfin' with Christian 'Urim' Tennyson is creating a very mystical and mythical jewel

The opening stanzas from *THE ODYSSEY* (an epic)

Homer 9th Century BC
Translated by Alexander Pope 1688-1744

The man[1] for wisdom's various arts renowned,
Long exercised in woes, O Muse! resound;
Who, when his arms had wrought the destined fall
Of sacred Troy, and razed her heaven-built wall,
Wandering from clime to clime, observant strayed,
Their manners noted, and their states surveyed,
On stormy seas unnumbered toils he bore,
Safe with his friends to gain his natal shore:[2]
Vain toils! their impious folly dared to prey
On herds devoted to the god of day;[3]
The god vindictive doomed them never more
(Ah, men unblessed!) to touch that natal shore.
Oh, snatch some portion of these acts from fate,
Celestial Muse! and to our world relate.

Now at their native realms the Greeks arrived;
All who the wars of ten long years survived;
And 'scaped the perils of the gulfy main.
Ulysses,[4] sole of all the victor train,
An exile from his dear paternal coast,[5]
Deplored his absent queen and empire lost.

---

1 The man: referring to Ulysses mentioned later
2 natal shore: *n.* hometown; the place of birth
3 god of day: the Greek sun god Hyperion, whose cattle Ulysses's men ate and were cursed to wander the Aegean Sea aimlessly
4 Ulysses: the Latin name for Odysseus
5 All were able to return home except for Ulysses

Calypso[6] in her caves constrained his stay,
With sweet, reluctant, amorous delay;
In vain-for now the circling years disclose
The day predestined to reward his woes.
At length his Ithaca[7] is given by fate,
Where yet new labors his arrival wait;
At length their rage the hostile powers[8] restrain,
All but the ruthless monarch of the main.[9]

6 Calypso: a nymph and the daughter of Atlas; she kept Ulysses captive as her husband on her island for seven years

7 Ithaca: the native home of Ulysses

8 hostile powers: the gods

9 ruthless monarch of the main: Neptune, who was the only god not to forgive Ulysses for his sin of blinding Polyphemus, Neptune's son. Neptune's curse is the main cause of Ulysses's wandering the seas for ten years

ROBIN HOOD AND THE SCOTCHMAN (a ballad)

Collected by Francis James Child 1825-1896

Now bold Robin Hood to the north would go,
With valor and mickle[1] might,
With sword by his side, which oft had been tried,
To fight and recover his right.

The first that he met was a jolly stout Scot,
His servant he said he would be;
"No," quoth[2] Robin Hood, "it cannot be good,
For thou wilt prove false unto me.

"Thou hast not been true to sire or cuz;"[3]
"Nay, marry,[4]" the Scot he said,
"As true as your heart, I never will part;
Good master, be not afraid."

But e'er[5] I employ you," said bold Robin Hood,
"With you I must have a bout;"
The Scotchman replied, "Let the battle be tried,
For I know I will beat you out."

Thus saying, the contest did quickly begin,
Which lasted two hours and more;
The blows Sawney[6] gave bold Robin so brave

1 mickle: *adj.* old form meaning 'great'
2 quoth: *v.* old form meaning 'said'
3 sire or cuz: father or cousin
4 marry: *interj.* old form indicating surprise or astonishment
5 e'er: *adv.* a literary form of 'ever'

The battle soon made him give o'er.[7]

"Have mercy, thou Scotchman," bold Robin Hood cried,
"Full dearly this boon[8] have I bought;
We will both agree, and my man you shall be,
For a stouter I never have fought."

Then Sawny consented with Robin to go,
To be of his bowmen so gay;
Thus ended the fight, and with mickle delight
To Sherwood they hasted away.

---

6 Sawney: a derogatory word for a Scottsman
7 o'er: *prep.* a literary form of 'over'
8 boon: *n.* favor

LUCY GRAY (a lyrical ballad)

William Wordsworth 1770-1850

Oft I had heard of Lucy Gray:
And, when I crossed the wild,
I chanced to see at break of day
The solitary child.

No mate, no comrade Lucy knew;
She dwelt on a wide moor,
—The sweetest thing that ever grew
Beside a human door!

You yet may spy the fawn at play,
The hare upon the green;
But the sweet face of Lucy Gray
Will never more be seen.

"To-night will be a stormy night—
You to the town must go;
And take a lantern, Child, to light
Your mother through the snow."

"That, Father! will I gladly do:
'Tis scarcely afternoon—
The minster-clock has just struck two,
And yonder is the moon!"

At this the Father raised his hook,
And snapped a faggot-band;[1]
He plied his work;—and Lucy took

The lantern in her hand.

Not blither[2] is the mountain roe:[3]
With many a wanton[4] stroke
Her feet disperse the powdery snow,
That rises up like smoke.

The storm came on before its time:
She wandered up and down;
And many a hill did Lucy climb:
But never reached the town.

The wretched parents all that night
Went shouting far and wide;
But there was neither sound nor sight
To serve them for a guide.

At day-break on a hill they stood
That overlooked the moor;
And thence they saw the bridge of wood,
A furlong[5] from their door.

They wept—and, turning homeward, cried,
"In heaven we all shall meet;"
—When in the snow the mother spied
The print of Lucy's feet.

Then downwards from the steep hill's edge

1 faggot-band: *n.* a match
2 blither: *adj.* joyous
3 roe: *n.* a deer
4 wanton: *adj.* frolicsome
5 furlong: *n.* 200 meters

They tracked the footmarks small;
And through the broken hawthorn hedge,
And by the long stone-wall;

And then an open field they crossed:
The marks were still the same;
They tracked them on, nor ever lost;
And to the bridge they came.

They followed from the snowy bank
Those footmarks, one by one,
Into the middle of the plank;
And further there were none!

—Yet some maintain that to this day
She is a living child;
That you may see sweet Lucy Gray
Upon the lonesome wild.

O'er rough and smooth she trips along,
And never looks behind;
And sings a solitary song
That whistles in the wind.

The beheading scene from *SIR GAWAIN AND THE GREEN KNIGHT* (a romance)

Translated by Bill Stanton

> A mysterious giant green knight has arrived at King Arthur's Court on Christmas Eve, riding upon a horse and carrying a large axe in one hand and a branch of holly in another.

Arthur stood watching adventure advance
and answered quickly as honor bid, neither awed nor afraid,
saying, "Wanderer, know you are welcome here.
dismount, if you may; make merry as you wish,
and we may learn in a little while what you would like."
"So help me God who sits on high," he said, "No."
"It is not my purpose to pass any time in this place.
But I have been told that your reputation towers to heaven:
that your court and castle are accounted the finest,
your knights and their steeds as the sturdiest in steel,
the best, the boldest, the bravest on earth,
and as fitting foes in any fine sport.
True knighthood is known here, or so the tale runs,
which is why I have come calling today.
You may be sure by this branch that I bear
that I come in peace, with no plans for battle.
I have a hauberk[1] at home, and a helmet too,
and other weapons I know well how to wield.
Yet as war is not my wish I am wearing soft silk,
but, if you are as bold as men believe you to be,
you will be glad to grant me the game that is mine
by right."

---

1 hauberk: *n.* chainmail armor

Then Arthur said, "I swear,"
"most courteous, noble knight,
if you'd like to battle bare,
you'll not fail to find a fight."

"Never fear," he said, "I'm not fishing for a fight
with the beardless children on the benches all about.
If I were strapped on steel on a sturdy horse
no man here has might to match me.
No, I have come to this court for a bit of Christmas fun
fitting for Yuletide[2] and New Years with such a fine crowd.
Who here in this house thinks he has what it takes,
has bold blood and a brash head,
and dares to stand his ground, giving stroke for stroke?
Here! I shall give him this gilded blade as my gift;
this heavy ax shall be his, to handle as he likes.
and I shall stand here bare of armor, and brave the first blow.
If anyone's tough enough to try out my game,
let him come here quickly and claim his weapon!
I give up all rights; he will get it for keeps.
I'll stand like a tree trunk—he can strike at me once,
if you'll grant me the right to give as good as I get
in play.

But later is soon enough,
a full year and a day.[3]
Get up, if you think you're rough,
let's see what you dare to say!"

If at first he had stunned them, now they sat stone-still:

2 Yuletide: *n.* Christmas time

3 The Green Knight offers any knight to cut off his head, if he can then cut off the knight's head a year later! A strange challenge indeed.

the whole hall, both high and low.
The mounted man moved in his saddle,
glared a red glance grimly about,
arched his bushy brows, all brilliant and green,
his beard waving as he waited for one man to rise,
to call or came forward. He coughed loudly,
stretched slowly, and straightened to speak.
"Hah! They call this King Arthur's house,
a living legend in land after land?
Where have your pride and your power gone,
your bragging boasts, your big words?
The glories and triumphs of the Round Table
have toppled at the touch of one man's words!
What? Fainting with fear, when no fight is offered?"
He let out a laugh so loud that Arthur winced
with shame; the blood shot to his flushed face
and churned

with rage and raised a storm
until their hearts all burned.
All king in face and form,
he reached that rider, turned,

and said, "Look here, by heaven! Have you lost your mind?
If you want to be mad, I will make you welcome!
Nobody I know is bowled over by your big words,
so help me God! Hand me that ax—
I will grant you the gift you beg me to give!"
He leaped lightly up and lifted it from his hand.
Then the man dismounted, moving proudly,
while Arthur held the ax, both hands on the haft,
hefted it sternly, considered his stroke.
That burly man bulked big and tall,

a head higher than anyone in the house.
He stood there hard-faced, stroking his beard,
impassively watching as he pulled off his coat,
no more moved or dismayed by his mighty swings
than anybody would be if somebody brought him a bottle
of wine.

Gawain, sitting by the queen,
could tell the king his mind:
"Lord, hear well what I mean,
and let this match be mine."

[…]

"Gad!" the Green Knight said. "Sir Gawain, I am glad
that your fist will fetch me the fun I hoped to find.
You have quickly retold in trustworthy words
a correct account of the contract I asked of the king,
save one stipulation that I must state: let it stand as your oath
that you will seek me yourself, and search anywhere
you feel I may be found to fetch back the same wages
I am paid today before this proud court."
"Where should I look?" Gawain asked, "Where do you live?"
"By Him that made me, your house is not known to me,
neither do I know you, knight, nor your court nor your name.
But teach me truly, tell me where to find you
and I shall work my wits out to win my way there.
I give my plain promise; I pledge you my word."
"That is enough for a New Year's pledge; you need say no
more,"
— So the green man answered gracious Gawain —
"If I'm telling the truth, why, when I've taken your tap,
and you've lopped me lovingly, you'll learn at once
of my house and my home and how I am named.

Then you can try my hospitality and be true to our compact.
Or I'll have no words to waste, which would be well for you:
you'd relax in this land, and not look for me further.
But stop!

Take up the grim tool you need,
and show me how you chop."
"Gladly, sir," he said, "Indeed,"
and gave the ax a strop.

The green knight got ready, feet firm on the ground;
leaned his head a little to let the cheek show,
and raised the rich riot of his hair
so the nape of his neck was naked and exposed.
Gawain held the ax high overhead,
his left foot set before him on the floor,
swung swiftly at the soft flesh
so the bit of the blade broke through the bones,
crashed through the clear fat and cut it in two,
and the brightly burnished edge bit into the earth.
The handsome head fell, hit the ground,
and rolled forward; they fended it off with their feet.
The red blood burst bright from the green body,
yet the fellow neither faltered nor fell
but stepped strongly out on sturdy thighs,
reached roughly right through their legs,
grabbed his graceful head and lifted it from the ground,
ran to his horse, caught hold of the reins,
stepped in the stirrup, strode into the saddle,
the head dangling by the hair from his hand,
and seated himself as firmly in the saddle
as if he were unhurt, though he sat on his horse without
a head.

He swiveled his bulk about;
the ugly stump still bled.
They gaped in fear and doubt
because of the words he said.

For he held the head up evenly in his hand,
turned the face toward the top of the high table,
and the eyelids lifted and looked on them all
while the mouth moved, making these words:
"Gawain, get ready to go as you have promised,
Seek me out, sir; search till you find me
as sworn here in this hall where all these knights heard.
I charge you, come as you chose to the Green Chapel to get
as good as you gave — you've got it coming
and will be paid promptly when another year has passed.
Many men know me as the Knight of the Green Chapel,
so search faithfully and you'll not fail to find me.
Come, or be called a faithless coward!"
He roared like a raging bull, turned the reins,
and drove for the door, still dangling the head,
while fire flashed from the horse's feet as if its hooves were flints.
Where he went no one knew,
nor could they name the country he came from nor his kin.
What then?

The king and Gawain grinned
and laughed at the Green Knight when
they knew full well it had been
a portent to their men.

APPENDIX

STUDY QUESTIONS

STUDY QUESTIONS FOR ELEMENT ONE: VOICE

GENERAL STUDY QUESTIONS

1. In groups of three or four, each student will choose any poem from the book. After reading the poem to the group, discuss the speaker's tone and ideas that he or she is trying to convey.

2. Individually, read the same poem several times. During your reading, take notes of three or four words, phrases, or images that you find important to understanding the tone. You must be able to explain why you think this is.

3. After preparation, you may either record a recitation of the poem, reading with an emphasis on the intended poem. For example, if the poem is tragic, read with an emphasized tone of voice. Or if there is time in class, you may stand up and read it in the same manner before the class.

4. For each poem in this chapter, decide what the speaker's tone is and give examples from the poem to support your answer.

MY LAST DUCHESS

1. According to the tone of the poem, how does the duke reveal himself? In other words, what kind of a man is he?

2. This poem is an example of poetical dramatic monologue. Here the reader understands a certain situation through the Duke's point of view. Reread the poem. Who is the poem about, the Duchess or the Duke?

3. Remember that a dramatic dialogue is heard only through the voice

of a character, as if listening to a person talk on the telephone. The idea is to use a point of view different from your own. Browning was neither domineering of women nor a murderer, yet that is the voice he took in "My Last Duchess."

THE RIGHTS OF WOMEN

1. This poem has the speaker address the reader directly. Since the poem is addressing women, are men excluded from the reading? Why or why not?

2. The aim of poetics of sensibility found in the writings of the women poets of the romantic period is to affect through sympathy and not by imitation. Women poets are sympathetic to distress and victimization with a profound emotion of being themselves disposed. Anna Barbauld challenges male dominated values by portraying an alienated sensibility through the call to arms of battle. What is it that women of the nineteenth century were fighting? How does the tone of the poem showcase the plight of these women?

3. Late eighteenth-century middle and upper class English women were taught to be primarily concerned with arousing and sustaining male sexual desire in order to capture a husband upon whom their financial welfare depended. They were obsessed with their personal appearance, beauty, and fashion. Mary Wollstonecraft launched a passionate plea for women's education in her *A Vindication for the Rights of Women* (1792). Wollstonecraft suggests that only if women were educated as fully as men, they would be able to realize their innate capacities for reason and moral virtue. Much of *A Vindication for the Rights of Women* is devoted to illustrating the damage caused by this gender definition of women's nature and social roles as essentially sexual. Of course, Wollstonecraft's call for a "revolution in female manners" was not the first feminist tract to be published in England, nor would it be the last.

What is Barbauld, who has taken on the persona of her speaker, trying to say in "The Rights of Women"?

4. Is the poem just as relevant today as it was then, or is the poem now considered dated and overly militant?

ON MY FIRST SON

1. This is one of the occasions where the speaker and poet are the same. This is known as the autobiographical "I". What has happened to Ben Jonson's son?

2. In what part of the poem do the father's feelings become exposed the most?

3. Are his thoughts and feelings consistent throughout the poem? In what part of the poem do they become different?

O CAPTAIN! MY CAPTAIN!

1. This poem is an example of an apostrophe (Element Three), where the speaker addresses a person not present. To whom is the speaker addressing?

2. Whitman's poem is said to also form an image, also known as **a concrete poem**. What image do you see in the poem? How does this image fit with the overall meaning of the poem?

3. How does the image of a ship and captain fit with the overall tone of the poem?

THE LOVE SONG OF J. ALFRED PRUFROCK

1. How does starting a poem in a classical language (Latin) set the overall tone of the poem? How does the rest of the poem differ in tone from the Dante quotation?

2. T.S. Eliot wrote poetry with the voice of the masses. His clear-cut poesy reads like prose, void of ambiguity. Reread "The Love Song of J. Alfred Prufrock." Then go and read Andrew Marvell's "To His Coy Mistress" (Element Three). Some critics have pointed out the similarities between these poems. In what ways are they similar? What is the point of view of both poems? What are the speakers talking about in both poems? Now observe the language and tone in both. How do they differ? What images and symbols does Marvell employ in his poem to set the tone? What images and symbols does Eliot use to set the tone? Which poem is more powerful to you, the classical or the modern? Which is easier to understand?

3. How many voices are in this poem? State how many and give evidence from the poem to support your answer.

4. Would you say that the speaker of the poem is confident? Why or why not? Give evidence from the text to support your answer.

STUDY QUESTIONS FOR ELEMENT *TWO*: THEME

GENERAL STUDY QUESTIONS

1. For each poem in this chapter, decide what the theme is and give examples from the poem to support your answer. Remember that your answer should include a subject and a predicate.

ARS POETICA

1. What is Macleish trying to say about poetry?

2. How does he feel about poetry? Use examples from the poem to support your answer.

3. What do the last two lines of the poem say? How does the theme of the poem coincide with the rest of the poem?

ON THE LATE MASSACRE IN PIEDMONT

1. Milton's poem is of the suffering of innocents under war and especially of full scale slaughter. Remember it was the slaughter of a "heretical" sect by the Catholic Church, which was the current ruling institution in Europe. Is there a parallel with then and now? Could the suffering and killing of the Waldensians be paralleled to the suffering and killing of Muslims today? Explain.

2. This poem has multiple themes of war, religion, and vengeance. Which theme predominates this poem?

THERE WILL COME SOFT RAINS

1. What does this poem comment about the frailty of human life compared to the strength of nature?

2. Now that North Korea is threatening nuclear attacks, does the theme of this poem have any added resonance?

3. What can we actually learn from this poem?

THE CONVERGENCE OF THE TWAIN

1. What is Thomas Hardy trying to say about the culture of his time? How does that culture create loneliness and solitude?

2. The sinking of the *Titanic* killed 1500 people. It was tragic beyond belief. What do you notice is suspiciously missing from this poem? Why do you think Hardy never mentions this? How does this omission relate to the overall theme?

SONNET ON CHILLON

1. The opening line of Lord Byron's sonnet is very powerful. "Eternal spirit of the chainless mind." What do you think it means?

2. How does the first line set up the theme of the whole poem?

STUDY QUESTIONS FOR ELEMENT *THREE*: FIGURES OF SPEECH

DAFFODILS

1. Where does Wordsworth utilize personification and simile in this poem?

2. Where does he use hyperbole?

THE ROAD NOT TAKEN

1. What is the anticipation in this poem? What is the remorse?

2. How are the various figures of speech used to portray both?

3. The speaker suddenly stops at a fork in the road. What causes the pause? Explain. What does this say about the speaker?

SONNET 19

1. What figures of speech does Shakespeare use in this poem? Explain your answer with clear examples from the poem.

2. This poem is an apostrophe to time. How is time personified in this poem?

3. Why does the speaker reference a tiger? What other animal is mentioned? Why?

TO HIS COY MISTRESS

1. What is the speaker talking about in this poem? What is the theme?

2. Why does the speaker compare love to a vegetable?

3. Find and explain the hyperbole in this poem.

4. Is the speaker of this poem's goal the same or different than the speaker's goal in Donne's "The Flea" (Element One)?

5. Should these poems be considered anti-feminist poems? Why or why not? How should a woman react to such poems?

6. Do you think the women in either Marvell or Donne's poems will do what they are asked to do? Why or why not? Give details from the poem to support your answer.

FOG

1. Explain how the metaphor works in this poem.

2. This poem is very short, only two sentences. Can it even be considered a poem? Explain.

3. What are other parts of speech Sandburg employs in this short poem?

AH, SUNFLOWER

1. What figure of speech does Blake employ in this poem?

2. Is Blake talking about a sunflower or something entirely different? If the latter, what is it?

STUDY QUESTIONS FOR ELEMENT *FOUR*: DICTION

LONDON

1. What causes the speaker so much sorrow in this poem?

2. What denotation do "mind-forged manacles" have? Now, what connotations does it have?

3. What occupations does Blake mention in this poem? Why does Blake mention these occupations only? What connotations do they have?

CARGOES

1. This poem is full of exotic and mystical words. You may have to look at the footnotes or even the dictionary for the denotations. However, what words carry special connotations for you? Use these connotations to comment on your overall feeling of the poem.

2. Each stanza of this poem gives a different view of cargo ships through the ages. Give labels to each stanza of cargo. In other words, what kind of cargo is each ship carrying? What does that have to say about the country it is going to?

ON FIRST LOOKING INTO CHAPMAN'S HOMER

1. Compare the language in this poem with that in "Cargoes." What is the language trying create in the reader's mind?

2. Look at the following words. What are the denotations of them?

Explain the connotations they hold for you in the context of the overall poem: bard, fealty, wide expanse, deep-browed, pure serene, watcher of the skies, eagle eyes, wild surmise.

3. After the exercise in question two, can you see how important not only the denotation of a word is, but also the connotation? Explain your answer.

IT IS A BEAUTEOUS EVENING

1. How does the diction in this poem differ from the previous two poems?

2. Read William Blake's poem "Sick Rose" (Element Six). Compare Blake's poem with Wordsworth's. Both speak of passing from a world of innocence into a world of experience. Which poem relates this idea better? Explain. How do these poems complement each other in this theme?

MINIVER CHEEVY

1. If "Miniver loved the days of old," what words in the poem illustrate this?

2. Look at all the verbs used in the poem. Do they point to Miniver's action or inaction? What does such diction reveal about character?

3. There is a running commentary on fame (mentioned as 'renown' in the poem), romance, art, and nobility (for "Miniver cursed the commonplace"). What is Miniver's view of these ideas? How do the words the speaker chooses reflect the mood of our times with that of the past?

JABBERWOCKY

1. Why does Lewis Carroll make up so many words for this poem?

2. Is this poem, in fact, a gibberish poem, or does it have more to say? Explain your answer.

3. Decide what the connotations of the words in italics are. Since many of the words are gibberish, erase the words in italics and make your own translation that fits with the overall context of the poem. Share your new poem with the class. Notice how much connotation matters in poetry.

A VALEDICTION: FORBIDDING MOURNING

1. In the first line of the poem, Donne says, "As virtuous men pass mildly away." Why do you think Donne would say that virtuous people have a mild death?

2. What is the meaning behind the comparison of virtuous men dying a mild death in the first stanza to the parting of lovers?

3. Donne refers to everyone else as laity, a congregation in the church. What is he saying about the relationship between him and his wife?

4. Donne incorporates a superb metaphor at the end of the poem. He compares the relationship of him and his wife to a compass, a tool to measure distance on a chart. Explain how this relationship works. What is the denotation of the compass? What is the connotation?

HOW DO I LOVE THEE

1. Both "A Valediction" and this poem were written by poets to their spouses. Donne was already married; Browning was engaged. In what ways is the diction the same? In what ways is it different? Does one poem register the concept of love greater than the other?

2. After Wordsworth, poets had tried to bring their poetry down to a baser level, to make their poems resonate with the masses. What language does the poet use to give it a more archaic feeling? Yet, if the language is archaic, why is it still a popular love poem, even today?

STUDY QUESTIONS FOR ELEMENT *FIVE:* IRONY AND PARADOX

ROMANCE

1. How does the Orwell create irony in this poem?

2. Identify the sarcasm in this poem?

3. What is the meaning of the title and why is it ironic? How does irony develop the theme of a poem? What is the theme of this poem?

HOLY SONNET XIV

1. How does irony work in this poem?

2. Explain the sarcasm being used in this poem. Use specific quotes to support your answer.

3. Is the poet criticizing anything? If so, what?

4. Identify the oxymora in this poem.

TO THE VIRGINS

1. Where does Herrick utilize paradoxical images?

2. How do such paradoxes comment on the speaker's perspective of love?

3. What is it about this poem that does not fit with other conventions

of love poetry? Look at Marvell's "To His Coy Mistress," Donne's "Valediction," and Browning's "How Do I Love Thee" to see if you can find the difference. Is there a difference? Explain.

THE WAYFARER

1. What is ironic about the pursuit of truth in this poem?

THE MARRIAGE OF HEAVEN AND HELL

1. The title is obviously ironic and oxymoronic. What does it mean?

2. Is this poem similar or different in theme with "The Wayfarer"? Explain.

3. What is Blake's ironic comment on the perilous path?

4. Explain what happened to the just man from beginning to end. Why would the villain leave the "path of ease" to drive the just man away from the "barren climes"?

RAINBOW

1. Wordsworth creates a paradox with the line, "The Child is father of the Man." What is he trying to say here?

STUDY QUESTIONS FOR ELEMENT *SIX*: SYMBOLISM AND ALLEGORY

THE TYGER

1. What does the tiger symbolize?

2. Is it only a terrifying creature? Explain why or why not?

3. Why does the creation of the tiger seem so mechanical? What allegory is Blake trying to create here?

KUBLA KAHN

1. "Kubla Kahn" is full of imagery. What are some symbols you get from these images? Use the poem to support your answer.

2. Look at the images of the pleasure dome, the caves, and the damsel with a dulcimer. What do these images have in common symbolically?

3. How does a historical figure like Kubla Kahn fit into the overall symbolism of this poem? In other words, is Coleridge trying to create a fantasy out of reality, or vice versa? Explain.

SAILING TO BYZANTIUM

1. What is being contrasted in this poem? What is the problem?

2. What symbols does Yeats employ to solidify this contrast?

3. What is the solution to the overall problem?

VIRTUE

1. Why is the poem called virtue?

2. What is the symbolism behind the sweet day, rose and spring?

3. Explain the juxtaposition between life and death in this poem.

UPHILL

1. What are the symbols of this allegory, and what do they represent (for example, the road and the hill)? How do the symbols combine to create the allegory? What is the allegory?

2. There are two speakers in this poem. Who are they and what are they discussing?

FIRE AND ICE

1. What does the fire and ice symbolize in this poem?

2. What is Frost trying to say by writing about polar opposites?

STUDY QUESTIONS FOR ELEMENT *SEVEN:* SYNTAX

GENERAL QUESTION

1. Find inverted syntax in this chapter's poems and see if you can rewrite them into a proper syntax.

2. Find examples of ellipses in these poems.

3. Choose a poem and rewrite it with varied syntax and punctuation to change its meaning.

THE GREAT FIGURE

1. How is Carlos's word order related to the situation the poem describes? What does Carlos gain by ordering his words the way he does?

2. The poem is one sentence. Why does Carlos break each line where he does? Is there any significance to this or is it just random? Rewrite the poem, breaking the lines in different places and see if it breaks the rhythm or even the feel of the poem.

I HEARD A FLY BUZZ

1. What purpose do all the dashes serve in this poem? Rewrite the poem without the dashes? Is the poem as effective? What is missing without the dashes?

2. The breaks in the syntax by way of dashes have a psychological effect. Read the poem out loud. What do such breaks in the syntax suggest about the speaker's state of mind?

3. How do the breaks in syntax highlight the theme?

WHEN I WAS ONE-AND-TWENTY

1. Why is the age of the speaker written in inverted syntax? What significance does this hold with the theme of the poem?

2. What is the advice that the wise man gives the speaker at the beginning of the poem? What advice does he give later? Why is there a contradiction? Is this contradiction important to understand? Explain.

POETRY

1. How does the speaker feel about poetry?

2. Is the poem just prose written as a poem (sentences broken up into lines and stanzas), or is there really something poetic about it? Explain.

3. Moore revised this poem repeatedly over the years since it was written[1]. In 1967, she reduced the poem to just three lines:

   I, too, dislike it.
   Reading it, however, with a perfect contempt for it, one discovers in
   it, after all, a place for the genuine.

   The one in this book is the 1921 version (often called the "original version"). How well does her poem fit into the notion of poetry? Does the fluidity of her lines match her idea of poetry? Explain.

---

1 see the webpage http://www.slate.com/id/2221785/sidebar/2221788/ for a couple of revision examples

4. Why would she revise her poem so many times in her lifetime? Is there a problem with the original?

IN JUST-

1. Explain how the syntax adds to the theme of the poem.

2. Read the poem out loud. How does the poem sound? Do you notice that the sound of the poem complements the theme? Explain.

3. Try rewriting the poem with different breaks in syntax? Can you still create the beat and sound of dancing and skipping?

I SHOT GATSBY

1. The speaker of the poem reveals a lot about himself. Is there a correlation between the syntax and the state of emotion the speaker is in? Explain.

2. The phrase "I shot Gatsby" is mentioned at the very beginning. Why do you think it is mentioned first?

STUDY QUESTIONS FOR ELEMENT *EIGHT:* IMAGERY

ODE ON A GRECIAN URN

1. What does Keats mean by calling the urn the "still unravished bride of quietness"? What images does this phrase conjure in your mind?

2. What is the meaning behind "beauty is truth, truth beauty"? What is Keats saying about art? About nature?

3. Draw a rough sketch of what this urn looks like. What is its shape? What is painted on it? Compare your sketch with other students. Are they similar or different? After the comparison, what kind of imagery does Keats employ, concrete or abstract? Explain.

THE LAKE ISLE OF INNISFREE

1. Capturing the five senses is a difficult feat in writing. How many of the five senses does Yeats capture in the poem? How do they add to the idea and emotion of the poem?

2. Describe if the poet predominantly uses concrete or abstract images in each stanza. Use examples from the poem to support your answer.

CHICAGO

1. What is the task Sandburg has set for himself in this poem? Why does he make us look at the ugly side of the city? Why is this important?

2. What images or details make the cityscape real for you? Were you

surprised when the poem reached a turning point in the last stanza? What is there to be proud of in that city?

3. What phrase or phrases are key to the concrete images of the cityscape? To the abstract images?

GOD'S GRANDEUR

1. How can the world "gather to a greatness, like the ooze of oil"?

2. What is God's grandeur? What images does Hopkins use to describe it? Would you say these are concrete or abstract images?

MEETING AT NIGHT

1. On just about every line, Browning creates images describing a man going to meet his lover. Identify each image. Which of the five senses does it arouse, and what feelings, either concrete or abstract, do you experience?

AMONG SCHOOL CHILDREN

1. Yeats uses classical art and myth to describe an encounter he had among school children. What are the images he uses?

2. Yeats is remembering this encounter when he was a young man. What effect do you think age and time has had on his remembrance of this encounter? Who is the teacher, and who is the student? Use excerpts from the poem to support your answer.

STUDY QUESTIONS FOR ELEMENT *NINE*: RHYTHM AND METER

TO AUTUMN

1. Identify the stresses and metrical feet in each line of this poem. Indicate the stresses on the poem in the book. Write the metrical foot next to each line.

2. Identify where the poet uses enjambment. Does Keats use catalexis in this ode?

CHARGE OF THE LIGHT BRIGADE

1. Note the meter used throughout the poem. It uses two stressed syllables, dimeter, followed by two unstressed syllables, dactyl. The first foot of each meter is stressed and then falls always making use of falling rhythm. Why would Lord Tennyson use this form in his poem? Read the poem out loud to hear and feel the falling rhythm and then imagine the scene it creates for you. What oral image is he trying to create?

2. Lord Tennyson wrote his poem ten years after the Crimean War. The situation was similar to the current war in Iraq; most of the British people did not want to participate in either war. Lord Tennyson wrote the poem to stir patriotism in the hearts of the people. Do you think this poem works to stir patriotism and favor for an unfavorable war? Explain. Do you think this poem would work to bolster favor for today's war? Why or why not?

THE LAMB

1. Notice how the poem is indented. The first and last two lines of

both stanzas are indented. Why?

2. The third line of the second stanza reads, "He is callèd by thy name." How many stresses (feet) are in this line? How can you tell? How does Blake show us there are this many stresses?

SHE WALKS IN BEAUTY

1. Identify the stresses and metrical feet in this poem. Indicate the stresses on the poem in this book. Write the metrical feet next to each line. Where is enjambment used?

2. How does Lord Byron define beauty in this poem? Is he in love with the woman, or is he simply celebrating her beauty? Use evidence from the poem to support your answer.

DULCE ET DECURUM EST

1. Indentify where Owen uses catalexis. How does the use of catalexis add to the reading of the poem? How is the meter of the poem supposed to read? Does the catalexis break this rhythm? Why or why not?

2. Explain the irony of this poem. According to this poem, is it "sweet and fitting to die for one's country"? Why or why not? Use excerpts from the poem to support your answer.

STUDY QUESTIONS FOR ELEMENT *TEN:* POETIC STRUCTURE

GENERAL STUDY QUESTIONS

1. Indicate the proper rhyme scheme next to each line of the poems in this unit.

2. Identify which poems in this unit are an English (Shakespearean) sonnet, Italian (Petrarchan) sonnet, a villanelle and a Spenserian stanza. The rhyme schemes should help you with this.

I DREAMED IN A DREAM

1. What kinds of structures does Whitman use in his poetry? Why might he be using these rather than traditional structures like rhyme?

2. How does the speaker in the poem feel? What is the speaker's attitude toward the listener?

THE HOUSE ON THE HILL

1. What is the speaker trying to say in this poem? What is the theme?

2. What stanza types are used in this poem? How does this help with the overall theme?

3. The rhyme scheme of this poem creates a half-serious and half-playful theme. What are the serious and playful parts of the poem?

THE FEMALE VAGRANT

1. Read this poem aloud. How does it sound? How aware are you of the meter and the line breaks following the rhyme words? When you concentrate on just the meter and rhyme, does the poem begin to sound mechanical? Explain.

2. Why is the poem entitled "The Female Vagrant"? Is this mentioned in the poem? Who is the speaker of the poem? What has happened to the speaker?

SUMMER DAWN

1. Identify the volta in this poem. How does this line introduce the turning point? What is the turning point? How does the poem lead up to this turning point?

2. Where does Morris break the traditional iambic pentameter of this poem? Why does he do this? How does it add to the theme?

MY LETTERS

1. Look at the rhyme scheme of this poem. Though the poem is one stanza, where do the stanza breaks actually occur? Identify the quatrain types being used?

2. What are some striking examples of enjambment? What is the purpose of using the ellipsis (...) in this poem? To what effect?

ODE TO THE WEST WIND

1. This poem is written in terza rima (an eleven syllable line arranged in tercets where the middle line of each tercet starts and finishes the rhyme in the following tercet). How does the use of terza rima add to the images of this poem? How is the stanza connected with the others in terms of metaphors, idea, and sound?

2. Notice the unusual syntax in the following lines: "Her clarion o'er the dreaming earth, and fill / (Driving sweet buds like flocks to feed in air) / With living hues and odors plain and hill." Rewrite the sentence into regular syntax so that it makes more sense.

STUDY QUESTIONS FOR ELEMENT *ELEVEN:* SOUND OF POETRY

GENERAL STUDY QUESTIONS

1. Read each of these poems out loud. How does studying this unit help you appreciate poetry better?

2. In each of the poems in this unit, identify all the rhyme types. Using different colored highlighters, mark them in the text and next to the line write what rhyme is being used.

A NOISELESS PATIENT SPIDER

1. Notice the rhythm of this poem. How does it affect you? Does the rhythm have anything to do with the theme?

2. What is the central theme of the poem (it is not the spider)? Why does Whitman start with the image of the patient spider?

3. You do not find out until halfway what the central theme is. What does Whitman gain or lose by waiting until this point to tell us his central theme?

ON JULIA'S VOICE

1. How does the sound of this poem compliment the theme?

DOVER BEACH

1. What is the central theme of the poem? Does the theme capture

your imagination? Are you able to see the images that Arnold has created?

2. How does the sound of the poem play into the theme and images?

LEDA AND THE SWAN

1. How is the theme of this Greek myth paralleled with the theme of the fall of Adam and Eve? In classical Greek myth, what caused mankind to stumble and fall? In Christian thought, what caused mankind to stumble and fall?

2. How is the rape of Leda by the swan treated in the first two stanzas? To help you answer this, pay attention to rhyme scheme and the overall use of rhyme. How does the poem sound? How does the sound of the poem complement or contrast the theme?

SONG

1. What is the theme of this poem? Why is the poem called "Song"? How do the last two lines of the poem fit into the overall theme?

2. Is this a positive or negative poem? How can you tell? How does the poem sound? Does the sound add to your notion of the positive or negative feeling of the poem? Explain.

STUDY QUESTIONS FOR ELEMENT *TWELVE*: POETIC TYPES

GENERAL STUDY QUESTIONS

1. Now that you have studied all twelve elements of poetry. Use your newly gained insight to analyze these deeply rich and highly stylized narratives. As you read each poem, take notes on the margins next each one, formulating ideas to help you experience the poems rather than just reading them.

2. How does understanding all twelve elements help you better understand these narrative poems? Can you see that narrative poems can be a mixture of great storytelling in every sense of the word (as compared to just fiction)?

3. What is your favorite narrative poem? Explain in detail.

4. What is your favorite lyric poem in this book? Explain in detail.

5. What is your favorite style of poem, the narrative or lyric? Explain in detail.

INDEX OF FIRST LINES

INDEX OF AUTHORS AND TITLES

– Reluctance
– Stopping by the Woods on a Snowy Evening
– The Road Not Taken
– The Silken Tent
Hardy, Thomas – The Convergence of the Twain
Herbert, George – The Collar
– Virtue
Herrick, Robert – To the Virgins
– On Julia's Voice
– Upon Julia's Clothes
Homer – The Odyssey
Hopkins, Gerard Manley – God's Grandeur
– Spring and Fall
Housman, A.E. – When I Was One and Twenty
Johnson, Ben – On My First Son
Keats, John – Ode on a Grecian Urn
– On First Looking into Chapman's Homer
– To Autumn
Kemp Owyne
Macleish, Archibald – Ars Poetica
Marvell, Andrew – To His Coy Mistress
Masefield, John – Cargoes
Milton, John – On the Late Massacre in Piedmont
– Paradise Lost
– When I Consider How My Light is Spent
Moore, Marianne – Poetry
Morris, William – Summer Dawn
Opie, Amelia – Song
Orwell, George – Romance
Owen, Wilfred - *Dulce et Decorum Est*
Pound, Ezra – In a Station in the Metro
Reeder, Steven Lynn – I Shot Gatsby
Robin Hood and the Scotchman
Robinson, Edwin Arlington – Miniver Cheevy
– The House on the Hill
Rossetti, Christina – Uphill
Sandburg, Carl – Chicago
– Fog

INDEX OF THIRTY SIX RECITED POEMS

Read by Steven Reeder
Recorded at Dongseo University Studio
Edited by Oksun Kang

Contents

Oksun Kang 강옥선

부산대학교에서 박사학위를 받았으며, 동서대학교 영어학과 교수로 재직 중이다.
저서 및 논문으로 『블레이크와 작은 천국』(동인, 2004, 공저), *Reading British Poetry* (동인, 2004, 공저), *The Close and Holy Darkness: Discovering Western Short Stories* (신아사, 2006, 공저), *Eternal Spirit of the Chainless Mind: 12 Themes in English Poetry* (신아사, 2007, 공저), *Exploring English Short Stories* (신아사, 2009, 공저), 「낭만기 여성시인의 도덕적 감수성 읽기」(2005), 「블레이크의 예언시와 사회의식」(2001) 등이 있다.

Steven Reeder

캘리포니아 주립대학교에서 석사학위를 받았으며, 동서대학교 전임강사(International Study Program)로 재직 중이다.
저서 및 논문으로 *Reading British Poetry* (동인, 2004, 공저), *The Close and Holy Darkness: Discovering Western Short Stories* (신아사, 2006, 공저), *Eternal Spirit of the Chainless Mind: 12 Themes in English Poetry* (신아사, 2007, 공저), *Exploring English Short Stories* (신아사, 2009, 공저), "Dracular as a Tragic Hero: The Illumination of Film on a Text" (2006), "Kicking Against the Pricks: The Vengeful Pursuit in Melvile's *Moby-Dick*", "Morally Chivalrous: Religious Irony in *Sir Gawain and the Green Knight*"(2008)

Elements of English Poetry

1판 1쇄 찍음 • 2011년 1월 25일
1판 1쇄 펴냄 • 2011년 2월 10일

지은이 • 강 옥 선 · 스티븐 리더
발행인 • 정 현 걸
발 행 • 신 아 사
인 쇄 • 예지인쇄

출판등록 • 1956년 1월 5일 (제9-52호)
서울특별시 은평구 녹번동 28-36 2F
전화 02.382.6411 • 팩스 02.382.6401
홈페이지 • www.shinasa.co.kr
이메일 • shinasa@chol.com

ISBN 978-89-8396-720-6 (93840)
정가 **11,000** 원